Reviews

The Medicine Man's Daughter

Carolyn F. Noell weaves a vivid, multi-colored tapestry of images and events that will quicken your emotions as she describes how Dayou Tucker, a thirteen-year-old daughter of a medicine man from Liberia, changed the lives of so many people in a small church community in Charlotte, North Carolina. As you read her words, you will be transported on a journey from the reality of life in war-torn Liberia through a teenager's physical and emotional struggle with hepatitis and the miracle of a liver transplant to the eternal hope we have through faith in Jesus. *The Medicine Man's Daughter* will help you to understand what the life-changing effects of giving unconditional love have on the lives of others as well as your own.
- Dale R. Harlan, Executive Director of Love in the Name of Christ of Mecklenburg County, N.C.

Carolyn Noell toggles back and forth between war-torn Liberia and an urban setting in the southern U.S. to tell a gripping story of human resilience, faith and community. Noell does a masterful job of integrating accounts of Dayou Tucker's African upbringing, the welcome she received from an inter-racial N.C. Baptist church, and the support with which she was surrounded as she faced end-stage liver disease and received an organ transplant.

As the spouse of a liver transplant recipient, I was particularly transfixed by Noell's grasp of this complicated journey. She and others walked beside Dayou when days and nights were long and challenging, and Noell conveys both the joy and the pain of the trek with honesty and grace.
- Lib McGregor Simmons, Pastor Davidson College Presbyterian Church

A poignant and captivating story that reveals not just one woman's courage, but that of a whole community of friends and strangers whose lives are changed forever by knowing one another.
- Jan Blodgett, archivist for Davidson College Library

THE MEDICINE MAN'S DAUGHTER

The Story of Dayou Tucker

a memoir by
Carolyn F. Noell

The Bridge
Huntersville, NC

Author's Note

This book is a work of creative nonfiction. While I've tried to portray the events of Dayou's story as accurately as possible, I have recreated conversations and summarized scenes.

ISBN-13: 978-0615975351

Produced in the United States of America

The Bridge
Huntersville, NC
www.TheBridgeBooks.com

This book is dedicated to Richard (R.J.) Toe

and to

Cassandra and Kelvin Drakeford,

who are parenting him.

Dear Ethel,
I hope you enjoy
this coming-of-age story.
Thanks for being a
friend for a long time.
Love,
Carolyn Noell

PREFACE

This is the story of Dayou, daughter of a tribal chief-medicine man and a woman named Sangay. At thirteen, she came to Charlotte, North Carolina from the edge of the rainforest in Liberia. It is the account of a child, who in a new country lived out her coming-of-age drama.

I, a retired teacher, shared some of this life with her, marveled at her will to survive, saw maturity flicker, then flame up. I entered her world as tutor, then became mentor and friend.

There were others who walked this path with us. In the lead or beside us or sometimes pushing from behind was Debra Hayes. This account will introduce many people who came to know and care about Dayou.

Readers may wonder if there are touch points between an older white lady and a young African girl. Racial lines dimmed over the years until I was referred to as one of her mothers. I tried to listen through time barriers and remember how it felt to be fifteen or eighteen or twenty-three. When she panicked, my mother instincts rushed in to calm and when she soared, my heart rose as a kite beside hers.

1

MOTHER'S MEDICINE

Bone Tired

*She's sick and
homesick,
and the shadows grow long,
counting down the days.*

May 19, 2005

I picked up the phone to hear Dayou's voice.

"Mrs. Noell, I want to go home to Liberia. I'm itching so bad I had to leave work yesterday because I scratched until I was bleeding. I stayed home today, but the itching is under the skin, in my body, and it's driving me crazy," Dayou continued. "I need to get some of the medicine my mother has. I need to bathe in it and drink it."

I imagine her mother going into the rainforest and cutting the bark of a tree with her knife, pounding and working juices from the tree skin.

"It won't be a cure, Dayou. You know that. Can't the doctors give you something?"

"No, they told me at the emergency room at Carolinas' Medical that there's nothing they can do. I want my mother here.

3

I have applied for a visitor's visa, but I can't wait much longer, so I want to go to her."

"Will it be safe? Elections are coming up and I hear the country's not stable."

"I'll be okay. I won't go to my village, just to my uncle's house in Monrovia. My mom will come there."

How could Dayou survive there? Monrovia had been crushed by civil war. Food was scarce. I didn't know about the water supply, and electricity was only on part time. Could her family care for someone as sick as Dayou?

During her teen years, I told Dayou when I had worries about her decisions. But she's an adult now, and I need to listen and accept. I don't think there's much time.

2

FIRST HOSPITAL STAY

Totota, Liberia – Charlotte

Rainforest birds dart into green,
Mama scrubs on river rocks,
bubbles rainbowing on brown arms.
Washing machines whir and click
in glittery buildings of glass and metal.

Father, in a white African shirt,
mixes medicine from plum bark,
second skin of a tree.
Doctors in green scrubs give an
anti-biotic, an anti-inflammatory.

Two worlds,
each growing
new leaves.

May 1996

I shouldn't have been surprised when the call came, but I was.
The signs were there.
Debra said, "Carolyn, Dayou's in the hospital."

I twisted the phone cord as I stared at Dayou's cheerleading picture: she was smiling, her hair smooth, pulled back, her body strong in the green sweater and short skirt.

"We were in Dr. Dawkins' office this afternoon," Debra said. Dayou's nose started bleeding. It was no little nosebleed. It was pouring. I had started toward her with paper towels when Dawkins came in pulling on gloves and yelling, 'Get back! Don't touch the blood! She has hepatitis, and she's not clotting.'"

The word *hepatitis* startled me but Debra and I had heard it from Dayou before. She had told us, but we had pushed it to the backs of our minds. Neither of us knew much about the disease, except for the word *transplant*. We didn't know if that was even possible for a person with a green card. The diagnosis didn't fit the picture of the active, busy girl we knew.

Debra Hayes was the social worker at our church, Briar Creek Road Baptist. Last week, after Dayou had complained of stomach pains and diarrhea, Debra had taken her to the doctor. Today was a follow-up visit.

"Dayou screamed and we had a hard time calming her," Debra said. "I took her to the emergency room at Mercy. They admitted her about an hour ago."

I rubbed my neck where it had begun to tighten.

"They'll call in the liver specialist, Dr. Rheindollar. I'll be back over there tomorrow."

"I'll be there, too," I said.

"Don't rush—not before noon. Dr. Rheindollar will have to see her first. Then there'll be a bunch of tests. You know how it goes."

"Yeah, thanks for calling, Debra. I'll see you at the hospital."

I stepped out on the screened porch hearing traffic sounds in spring twilight as I thought about my times with Dayou. I began tutoring her last year when she was in eighth grade. She was fourteen, eleven when she left Liberia and thirteen when she got a visa to the U.S. from Ivory Coast. The president of Liberia, Samuel Doe, had been killed, along with his cabinet, and the country was in the nightmare of war with shooting, torturing and raping. I'd been so glad Dayou got away. She'd had a lifetime of adjustments in three years. She didn't know if her family were alive. She'd already had to deal with a different school system, strange foods and American culture.

* * *

The car was warm from the spring sun as I merged into traffic on I-77. As I thought about Dayou, uneasiness slipped around me. James and Rebecca Tucker had brought her from Liberia to Charlotte. He had worked in Monrovia for the Voice of America, a radio station transmitting to most of Africa. His job was to keep the generators operating, and it insured a visa to America for him and his family when civil war broke out.

A few months after settling in Charlotte, James and Rebecca separated and Dayou chose to stay with James, who she called "uncle." James was in his mid-sixties and too tired after working two jobs to do much parenting.

Dayou had been happy at times. I remembered her smile last year when she handed me her report card showing she was on the B-honor roll and her excitement when she made cheerleader. Last May, the Charlotte City Council honored her for coming through hard times with a positive attitude. I'd helped her with homework and school projects, shopping for clothes; I listened while she talked about home. But what would be ahead? How would hepatitis affect her life? Would she be able to attend to school? Could she go places with the youth group at church? Would she be in bed all the time?

* * *

I found a parking place in the multi-level lot at the hospital, anxious to see Dayou, but scared, too. Cautiously I pushed open the door to her room. Her nose was bandaged and she was wearing a shapeless hospital gown.

"Hello," she said with a smile, but her eyes were sad. The area around the pupils was yellow. I went over to hug her. She felt solid, making the diagnosis harder to believe.

"What's going on?" I asked.

"Not much," she said, trying to sound casual. "I've just been lying here thinking about yesterday and wondering what's going to happen."

A young nurse with light brown skin pushed the door open. With one hand she touched her braids and in the other she carried a small box.

"My tool kit," she joked as she placed it on the bed.

"I hate to tell you, but I need some more blood."

"I thought I lost most of it yesterday afternoon," groaned Dayou.

"I can probably find more," the nurse said with a smile and a wink as she pushed up the sleeve of Dayou's hospital gown and pulled on gloves. Dayou made a fist and studied the flower-shaped ring on the woman's finger.

Dayou said, "They took blood in the emergency room and again last night. Is something wrong?"

"Not necessarily; this happens all the time. Have you been in the hospital before?"

Dayou shook her head. "Only to have tests, not to spend the night."

As the nurse took the cover off the needle, Dayou looked over at the clock.

"It's twelve and ROTC class is starting," she said. "Colonel Love will see my name on the absentee list and wonder where I am."

I visualized the busy scramble at West Charlotte High School as students changed classes and settled in as the tardy bell rang.

Dayou looked at me as she said, "There's only five weeks left in the school year. I don't want to mess up ninth grade by being in here. Will I be able to get my homework?"

"I can go to the school, talk to your teachers and get a student to bring your assignments. Don't worry; we'll figure out a way."

The nurse pressed a cotton ball on Dayou's arm and fastened it with tape. "Take care," she said before closing the door.

Turning to me, Dayou said, "Did Miss Debra tell you what happened in Dr. Dawkins's office?"

"She called last night and told me a little—mostly that you were sent here. What happened?"

"My nose started bleeding with huge clots that Miss Debra said looked like chicken livers. I was so scared I started screaming."

"Why did it scare you so much?"

"When I was a little girl, I had nosebleeds that didn't stop for days and I know it means I'm real sick. I was still shaking when Miss Debra put me in her SUV to bring me here."

Dayou's eyes showed fear and uncertainty. "I'm afraid I might be losing everything." Her voice broke and she wiped her eyes with a Kleenex she pulled from the small box on her table.

I touched her arm and we sat silent for a minute letting our touch speak what our words could not. I watched slices of sunlight on the tile floor, tiny bits that escaped through closed blinds.

Finally, Dayou broke the silence and in a matter-of-fact voice said, "The doctors cauterized my nose and packed it with gauze. It stings and burns; I am *so-o* tired."

With my hand on her arm, I asked, "Were you able to sleep last night?"

"They kept waking me up to check my pressure and temperature, and I had trouble going back to sleep. I'm not used

9

to these noises and people moving around after midnight. When I was awake, I thought about my mom and wished she was here," Dayou said.

I realized being in the hospital was scary for her. It upsets most people, but what was it like for her, a young girl away from family and her home country?

"Has Miss Debra been by?" I asked.

"Yes, she went to the church but said she'd be back later."

"Have you eaten anything?"

"They brought my breakfast on a tray with metal lids covering the plates. The eggs were yucky, so I just drank some juice and pushed it away. An aide tried to get me to eat some. I told her they were nasty. I said, 'They stink. Put the lid back on.' The aide clapped the top on my tray and walked mad when she left the room. I don't care. I'm not going to eat stuff I don't like."

This was vintage Dayou. She was feisty even when she was sick and scared. Sometimes I got impatient with her strong responses to people who tried to help, and other times I realized this was a key to her survival.

* * *

Dayou's knees pushed up the counterpane and she rubbed the dents in the white material with her brown fingers. I stood to open the blinds. There was not much in her room except the bed and a tray table. A TV hung from the ceiling. There was a small closet and a bathroom with a shower. A cabinet made with light-colored wood sat beside the bed with her schoolbooks stacked on one end beside a pink teddy bear. A helium balloon nudged the ceiling above it. The floor was shiny tile and a large window framed new leaves on an oak tree.

Dayou saw me looking out and said, "I love that tree. It reminds me of home."

10

Since I'd known Dayou, I'd wished I could see the landscape in Liberia. Africa had long fascinated me, and Dayou's warm descriptions of home and the people she loved made me want to visit, the way a good book pulled you to walk on the land and meet the characters. I knew I couldn't go because the State Department had a warning on the Internet for American travelers. There was little police protection except in Monrovia, but I wanted to see the rain forest, birds, flowers, mango and rubber trees. I wanted to see the women washing clothes in the river, hear their singing and meet Dayou's father in his white African shirt.

I thought Charlotte must seem like hard surfaces of pavement, brick and glass compared to the greenness around Dayou's village.

Dayou sat up, interrupting my reveries as she leaned to the side to see what was going on in the hall. Families walked by, carrying flowers and plastic bags. Dayou's mother was thousands of miles away near Totota. Some of the women from our church, including Debra, Lois Bumpus and I tried to fill in. We saw that she had what she needed, but that was not even close to filling her mother's place.

Dayou had told me that when she walked from the school bus to the empty apartment, she'd thought, "If my mom were here, she'd ask what I learned in school today? If I showed her a good grade or told her something I'd done well, she'd say, 'I'm proud of you.' She'd hug me and say, 'I love you.'"

She said her mother would cook special things for her like rice with palm butter and spinach soup and the two of them would sit at the table and talk.

My own mother and I talked for hours when I was a teenager and her patient listening helped me get through the hard parts of growing up. We discussed school, what happened on the school bus, how to get through hard times with friends, where I'd go to college and what my major would be. I thought Dayou must miss this more than she even knew.

I turned from the window as Dayou said, "If my mother was here, she'd know what treatment to use. Growing up, I was sick a lot and she tried to help me when I had yellow jaundice. She put plantain leaves in cold water and bathed me with it. Mother used to squeeze some other leaves into water and make me drink it. The water was green."

"The medicine I hated most was one made with the second skin of a tree," Dayou continued. "I think it may have been plum bark. Mother beat it until it was a white liquid. It was not bitter or sour, just weird. It had some pepper in it, and it was so nasty that I hated to take it. Since my dad is a medicine man, I think mom learned cures from him."

I asked if she had ever been tested for hepatitis in Liberia.

She told me she had gone to a clinic when she was nine years old and they had taken blood samples just before she left to live in Monrovia, so she never got the test results. She said they had given her a big bottle of white pills that tasted horrible – so bitter she couldn't stand it. When she got to Monrovia, she didn't tell her half-sister about the medicine – she just never took it again.

I wondered if those *nasty* pills were quinine for malaria. I had always heard that its bitterness was almost beyond anything you could imagine.

Dayou turned in the bed adjusting her covers around her. With a weak smile and a twinkle in her eyes, she said, "Some of the kids from church came to see me last night." She pointed to the pink bear with a red bow around its neck. The "Get Well" balloon was tied to its arm and softly bumped the ceiling. "They brought the balloon and the bear. They stood around the bed and talked. Before they left, they prayed for me. It was nice."

As I picked up the bear and rubbed the satin ribbon, I noticed Dayou's frown.

12

"Mrs. Noell, they had to line up at the sink to wash their hands before they left the room."

She was silent a moment. "It reminded me of the lepers in the Bible – how they had to yell, 'Unclean' when people came close. Now, I understand a little how they felt – lonely, cut out, different."

"Dayou, do you think your friends were put off by having to wash their hands?"

"No, they laughed and joked about it, and I don't think they were worried about catching hepatitis, but I felt strange knowing I have something – something dangerous."

I put the bear back on the cabinet and sat in a chair beside her bed. My fingers smoothed the edge of the sheet, and I sensed she needed to say more.

Dayou's brown eyes were sad when she looked up at me. "I was diagnosed with hepatitis after I came to Charlotte. It scared me when I read about it in my science book because there is no cure except for a transplant. Do you think a girl from Africa can get a transplant?"

My hands tightened on the sheet and, having no answer, I looked down.

"If Dr. Rheindollar says I need surgery, what will happen? I don't want to die, not here. I want my family around me – their faces bending over me, watching. I want to be buried in Liberia. But more than anything, I want to live. I want to go to school, to be with my friends and do things with the youth group at church. I've struggled to get this far, coming all the way across the ocean, learning to do my schoolwork, surviving without my family."

She turned her head away. Her voice choked, "It doesn't seem fair to lose it all. I'm just sixteen."

Dayou was right. Life was not always fair, especially when young people were sick. My trust was in God's perfect love for us, despite a world that contains disease and bad judgment. Why her? Why now? I couldn't answer. I did believe God would be present with her no matter what happened. I visualized her as a little girl drinking water from the stream near her village with no worry about the possibility of getting sick.

I looked up as the nurse's rubber-soled shoes squeaked on the tile floor. She said, "Dr. Rheindollar has ordered a liver biopsy for tomorrow."

3

A NEW BEGINNING

Far-Away

I left home without pictures,
with stories, I try
to pull back images.
I couldn't live
if their faces were lost.

Dayou and I were silent for a few minutes while she processed the news that she would soon know how far her hepatitis had progressed.

The phone rang. It was Lady Dennis, Dayou's friend from Liberia, saying she had been to see Dayou's teachers and would bring her assignments by as soon as school was out.

To keep Dayou's thoughts from lingering on dark places, I suggested we start doing the homework that was due today. I pulled the tray table close, peered underneath to find the lever, and adjusted the height so she had a place to put her papers and to write.

Like all teenagers, Dayou was ready to switch tracks, and we worked on math for a while, then English grammar. Afterwards, Dayou called Debra and told her she was hungry for Chinese food. Debra promised to bring some tomorrow.

A nurse's aide came in to take Dayou's vital signs. Dayou watched the flashing numbers on the monitor and wondered aloud, "Does it mean I'm okay?"

"I don't understand the numbers either," I said. "Let's talk about home. What do you think your mother's doing right now?"

"She might be working in the field or coming in to cook supper. You know it would be five hours later over there. I wish I could taste rice again the way she fixed it. I wish I could hold my little brother."

"I know they would love to see you," I said.

I had always asked about her life in Africa. Dayou was hungry to tell about her family. She didn't have any pictures, so talking about home helped her hold on. She said she never wanted to forget because she couldn't stand it if she lost their faces. It had been five years.

Looking at my watch, I said, "Dayou, I've got to go, but I'll be back tomorrow."

As I moved toward the door, Dayou said, "Mrs. Noell, don't forget to wash your hands."

I felt heaviness in my chest as I stopped at the sink and turned on the water. I knew Dayou was watching as I soaped and moved my hands one over the other. I dried them with a paper towel, tossed it into the trash and pushed my glasses up. With a brief wave, I reached for the door handle. The lock clicked as I closed the door. My heels sounded too loud on the tile as I walked to the elevator.

* * *

Driving home, I remembered how I had met Dayou a year and a half ago. My husband Tom and I were helping with Autumn Fest at the church. Booths had been set up around the sides of the gym. A huge spider web swung from the center of the ceiling.

16

The floor in the fellowship hall was marked off with masking tape, and a cakewalk went on to the sound of recorded music. Squealing children in costumes ran through the building, while the smell of popcorn butter made the air delicious.

In this din and excitement, Debra spotted me manning a booth and asked to speak with me. "I saw your name and Tom's on the list of volunteers for after-school tutoring," she said. "Instead of working with the elementary kids, there is a middle school student here from Liberia, who needs your help. What do you think?"

Before I could answer, she went on.

"I would like you to work with her in the church library, while Tom and the others are in the children's building. Would you be willing to do that?"

I was hoping for a minimum commitment, such as listening to children read for forty-five minutes. This sounded like a different level of involvement. I have finally, after years of over-work, learned to protect *self* before committing to anything. With cautious interest, I said, "Tell me a little more about her."

"She's in the eighth grade at Piedmont Middle," said Debra. "The problem is that she came here two years ago when she was thirteen with limited schooling. At Crown Point Elementary, they put her in sixth grade. She struggles all the time to get basic skills."

A myriad of self-protecting questions ran through my mind like an express train. Did I want to deal with the angst and unpredictability of an eighth grader again? Did I have the time? I loved my freedom – well, what there was of it. Volunteer projects already filled my days.

I knew that many retired teachers were cautious about stepping into deep water again, but most of us can't resist being needed and challenges call us like a siren. As a teenager, I had felt God wanted me to be a missionary and had started college in pre-med, planning to work in Africa as a doctor. I changed course after a couple of chemistry classes. My grades were okay, but I was not as interested in the subject as I expected to be. When my professor asked me to be lab assistant the next year, I felt that position should go to someone who loved chemistry. I didn't. But maybe this was my chance to help an African girl and to do so on my own ground.

Still, I hesitated before answering Debra. Finally, I said, "Yes, I'll try."

Her broad smile indicated I had made the right decision. "Good," she said. "She's here tonight and I want you to meet her."

In a couple of minutes she came back with her arm around a teenage girl. She was much shorter than Debra – about five feet, three inches, with a stocky build. Her skin was dark, her hair pulled back into a ponytail and she wore jeans, sneakers and a sweatshirt. As Debra introduced her, the young African gave me a direct look before quickly glancing down. Her eyes were widely spaced and she had a strong jaw line with full lips. She didn't rush to talk, nor did she fidget. There was a serenity and dignity about her that left me feeling she had experienced much more than other girls her age.

"Dayou, this is Mrs. Noell, a retired teacher who is going to help you with your schoolwork on Wednesday afternoons. Will that be okay?"

Dayou's face lit up when she smiled, showing a space between her front teeth. She nodded. "Yes."

There was so much noise I had not understood her first name. "Please spell your name for me and I'll write it down." I pulled a pen and a scrap of paper out of my pocket. "I need to hear and to see in order to be able to remember."

"D-A-Y," she began. She spoke rapidly with a heavy accent, letters slurring together.

18

Superman and a witch wearing a mask ran yelling by us with fists full of popcorn. We laughed.

"I'm sorry. Could you spell it again?" I wrote the letters and stuffed the paper into my pocket. "Miss Debra tells me you go to Piedmont."

"Yes."

"I like that school. My three children went there, and I taught there for a short time. When would you like us to start working?"

Dayou shrugged. "Any time."

We settled on Wednesday at 3:30. I headed back to my booth and she to hers.

As dozens of costumed children came by my booth and I helped them with the game, my mind went back again and again to Dayou. I wondered what problems she was having and what kind of relationship we'd form. I was curious about her reading and math levels. I had never worked with a student who had missed most of elementary school. I had taught English and history in high school years ago, right out of college. Later my work was in middle school in career guidance and economics. I had no training for this challenge. Would I be able to help her learn missed skills and keep up with daily assignments? I knew I was not the ideal choice, but probably the only one available.

That night was our beginning.

My reminiscing about Dayou ended as I turned into the parking lot of the Food Lion in Cornelius. I pulled the key out of the ignition thinking life takes strange turns. I had never imagined tutoring would lead down a path that included hospital visits and concern about a family in Liberia whose names I couldn't spell.

4

WITH ROOTS IN AFRICA

Patterns on the Wall

Africa, shadow on the wall,
cradles Liberia where
a child is sick.
My father kills a chicken
to work the cure.
Blood spatters in the dust.

On the wall of Dayou's hospital room, a shadow created by
the moving leaves of the oak tree outside her window reminded
Dayou of her Africa. Her eyes traced the west coast and stopped
on the curve where the big jutting out part turns back. This was
Liberia, her country.

When Dayou was little, her mother lived in a big house with
stucco walls and a metal roof with all her father's wives. Her
father was a big man in Bong County, a tribal chief, but Dayou
didn't understand why her mother would be willing to share her
husband with other women.

Even though Dayou's mom was wife number three, she had
her own kitchen. All the other wives shared one. Wife number
one had one child, wife number two had two and Dayou's mom
had five.

21

Dayou remembered hearing her parents talking one morning. Her mother was angry and said, "Why did you tell the American lady she could take Dayou? I don't want her going to the States. We might never see her again."

Her father said, "I would miss her as much as you, but America is a wonderful place. People are rich there, and Dayou could have a chance to get an education. You know Americo-Liberians in Monrovia have always taken some village children to work for them, and some of them have been educated," he continued. "I just want to give our daughter a chance to have things we can't give her. A chance to go to America doesn't come every day."

"Why didn't you ask me?" her mother persisted.

"You weren't here. You had gone to your sister's and the lady wanted an answer. She'll pick her up this afternoon. Tell her to get her things together."

Dayou was excited because she had heard stories about life in the States. She thought it would be easy and people would walk around with their feet a few inches above the ground, like they were on a low-lying cloud. She daydreamed about big houses and pretty clothes while she ate some pineapple for breakfast. Her sister Nancy sat across from her looking sad. The girls were close and Nancy didn't want her to go.

"Let's go to the village, Dayou. This is our last day together. We'll be back before the Americans come."

Dayou didn't know if Nancy stalled on purpose, but they stopped at a friend's house on the way home. When they got within sight of their house, they spotted the car pulling away. They ran down the dirt road yelling, "Stop!" But the Americans never saw the girls through dust rolling up behind their car. Dayou and Nancy knew that Africans wait for things, and they thought Americans would too. Africans considered approximate times okay. The girls didn't have a clue how Americans value promptness. Dayou always wondered what her life would have been like if she'd gotten back a few minutes earlier.

* * *

When Dayou was born, Meatta Briggs, her mother's sister, who lived in Totota, had lost a baby a few months earlier. Dayou's mother had felt sad for her sister and had allowed her to take Dayou. Aunt Meatta loved children, so she raised Dayou and several of Dayou's cousins, who thought of their aunt as a second mother. Sometimes Meatta had to explain to others that her sister, Sangay Briggs, had given birth to Dayou. Dayou grew up between the two houses, always going to visit her mother and brothers and sisters.

The two houses were about a forty-five-minute walk apart. Dayou liked this because she was as strong willed as her mother, so when they had trouble getting along, Dayou would go back to her aunt's where she would be petted and given her favorite foods. She remained close to her father, staying with him from time to time, even after he and her mother were no longer together.

At the age of six, Dayou started going to school in Totota and soon hated it. The principal had a practice of waiting in front of the school to punish tardy students. He stood in the grass slapping a wooden paddle against his leg. Dayou's cousin made her wait for her and since her cousin was always late, that meant Dayou was paddled. She dreaded it.

When she was little, Dayou didn't like studying. Like most children, she spent more time playing than learning. In the mornings, when it was time to get ready for school, she cried. But her aunt made her go.

There were times when she was sick with yellow jaundice and nose bleeds. When she had to miss school, she fell behind, and it was hard to catch up.

In Liberia, you don't move on to the next grade until you pass the end-of-year exam. Since she didn't work hard, Dayou made little progress. But she was not embarrassed to be held back because there were lots of older children in the lower grades. Some parents didn't have the money for tuition until their son or daughter turned nine or ten. Regardless of age, they always started in kindergarten and stayed there until they passed the test.

Some people in the tribes were more interested in their young people going to the Sande Bush Society, where they were initiated into manhood or womanhood, than in sending them to traditional school. The rituals, passed on by oral tradition from one generation to the next, were secret. Her Aunt Meatta and her mother didn't approve of sending children to this society, but it had been important to some of Dayou's father's wives. One of those wives was in charge of Sande Bush, so Dayou had gone when she was eight instead of going to school. A lot of people loved the old tribal ways and didn't want to lose them.

* * *

Before the Civil War and before Dayou left Liberia, one of her sisters, who had sickle cell anemia, had a seizure and fell onto some fire coals that caused a bad burn on the back of her head. At that time their father was in another village. When her sister's head didn't heal, her mother wanted to take her to the hospital.

Dayou's mother walked to Aunt Meatta's in Totota and told her that her husband gave her ten dollars to take Dayou's sister to the hospital. Dayou can still hear her mother's strong voice saying, "That's not enough to pay for treatment at a hospital. I told him to keep his money. I'll take care of her myself."

That was when Sangay moved out of her husband's house. Dayou's father came to Meatta's and begged his wife to come back. Dayou's mother said, "The only time I will be with you will be after you go to my father's grave, and he tells you I should go back. After that, you must go to my mother's house and see if she tells you the same thing."

Still, Dayou's father came several times asking his wife to come home, which convinced Dayou he loved her mother. But Sangay always refused.

Her father made country medicine for people who couldn't afford to go to a hospital. Once when a child in their village ran a high fever, he was called. Dayou couldn't remember all the things he did, but she could still see him cutting off a chicken's head and the bird flapping all over the ground while everybody jumped back to get away from the blood spurting around their feet. After her father finished with his magic, they plucked the chicken and made soup.

Dayou said her father was a heavy man but not too tall, maybe five feet, six inches. He was now in his seventies. "He had so many women I wouldn't know how to guess the number. This was the crazy part – his wives would go out looking for girls who would stay with him until they were twenty-one, and then he would marry them. In each of his villages, he had a house with wives and lots of children." Dayou said she wondered how many brothers and sisters she had. She bet nobody knew. When she left there were twenty-one girls and maybe that many boys.

One night, Dayou's half-brother asked Dayou's sister to dance. They had not been together in so long they didn't recognize each other. People started laughing and told her he was her brother. She was so embarrassed she covered her face with her hands. When she finally looked up, he was gone. In Bong County, it was forbidden for a brother and sister to dance together.

The women told Dayou that when she got breasts, someone would come asking her to go live with an older man. Shaking her head, she cringed at the thought. "No, I'll never do that."

They said, "Yes, you will," and then laughed about it.

With fire in her eyes, Dayou said, "You'll see. That's something I'll never do."

Dayou's family had called her *mouthy* when she stood up for her rights. She told them she would go far away someday. Nobody believed her.

***

Was her family alive? Dayou believed they had made it through the war, but she didn't know how to find out. A lot of people had been killed, left home or even left Liberia, but she sensed her parents were still there in their part of Bong County.

Dayou felt that if her mom or dad had died, she would have known it deep in her soul. She would have felt a sense of loss, an empty place. She had a strong belief that if she could go home, she'd find them right where she'd left them.

5

SECOND CHANCE

Rebels in the City

Gunshots split
the warm night,
transformers explode.
From the beach I see
darkness in Monrovia.

The needle liver biopsy was scheduled for eleven o'clock. It was not a big operation, but Dayou was scared because she didn't think the news would be good.

Last night after supper Dayou said she felt low and wondered if she were going to die. She called Lois Bumpus, a member of our church who was a motherly friend, and asked her to spend the night at the hospital. Lois readily agreed to stay until morning.

Dayou's interracial church had become her family. About half the people who came to see her were white and half were black. Hospital staff occasionally asked Dayou about her church and she said, with pride, "It's Briar Creek Road Baptist, near the old coliseum."

The staff said they thought it was wonderful that the church was multi-cultural and that more congregations should be integrated. Even Dr. Dawkins, who was black, was curious about this. Debra was also black, while Dr. Rheindollar, Lois Bumpus, Pastor Dale and I were white. A church where race was a non-issue had been a dream of Pastor Dale Harlan's. He encouraged us to move toward more racial reconciliation. Some of us felt strongly that Sunday morning at eleven o'clock should not be the most segregated time of the week.

Being in a racially diverse congregation was a dream come true for me. Since I was in ninth grade, I had been arguing for civil rights. I never understood the artificial lines our society drew between races. People from different backgrounds brought an excitement to a classroom, church, or even a party.

Dayou said in Africa she had seen whites – none of them near her mom's house in the countryside, but a few white families lived in Totota. She remembered when she and her sister had tried to pick strawberries and grapes from a white man's garden and he had chased them out. He had come out of the house carrying a gun.

Sometimes, the Lutheran missionaries, whose church was near her Aunt Meatta's house, had other white families over for wiener roasts. Dayou said she and her cousins, who lived with Aunt Meatta, had stood where they could see them and wondered what hot dogs were made of and how they tasted, something she wouldn't find out until after she made her way to the United States.

The whites spoke English, as did the Liberians, and they ate most of the same foods, so the Liberians thought of the whites as equals.

When Dayou came to this country, she thought all African-Americans would be rich like some of the Americo-Liberians in Monrovia. She expected them to speak English and not a dialect. When she got here, she was astounded at how many Africans were struggling with speaking English. Not only were there Africans but also Hispanics, Jamaicans, Vietnamese and folks

28

from all over the world. She said her school reminded her of the United Nations.

The nurse came in to tell Dayou it was time for her to go downstairs for the biopsy. She felt shaky and as frightened as she had been during the civil war.

* * *

Charles Taylor's troops and Prince Johnson's men came into Monrovia on an August night in 1990.

Dayou did not understand why the rebels were fighting. Later, she learned that Charles Taylor and other rebel leaders wanted to get Samuel Doe out of office and swing the power over to themselves. Each rebel group had set up checkpoints throughout the country.

When Samuel Doe took office in 1980, he had been the first tribal man to be president and there had been lots of excitement. But now Dayou knew Samuel Doe had lost his power. The Americo-Liberians were the descendants of freed slaves from the U.S. who had founded a colony in Liberia in the 1800s and, from that time on, controlled the government. They had been the ones who had university education, money and authority. Some built plantation houses which were copies of the ones they had known in the States. For years they had little to do with the tribal peoples except to use them for labor.

By the late 1980s, more of the native people had an education and they had spoken out against what they thought was unfair treatment. There were rumors that President Doe could not read, at least not well, but the tribal peoples saw him as their champion.

Charles Taylor had gone to college in the United States. His father was an Americo-Liberian and his mother was from the Gola tribe.

29

On Christmas Eve of 1989, Taylor had come in from Ivory Coast with about a hundred men, moved through the country and in eight months was at Roberts Field, an airport outside Monrovia.

* * *

Dayou was in the city because, when she was nine, her dad had sent her to live with his niece so she could attend school. This relative did not like children and had not bothered to enroll Dayou in school. Miserable, Dayou had moved in with her half-sister Mary who had a family of her own. A friend of Mary's, who had liked Dayou, invited her to stay with her at her house. Mary's friend was good to Dayou and treated her like her own daughter.

One week before the troops entered Monrovia, the lady who had taken Dayou into her home heard rumors and prepared to go to Guinea, where she had grown up. She asked Mary if Dayou could go with her, but Mary said, "No." Dayou was ten and not allowed to decide for herself.

After the lady left, Dayou stayed on for a while. The lady's husband didn't leave with his wife. Their house was near the beach, west of the city, and that's where Dayou was when the lights went out.

She had gone outside and looked to the west. The lights on the beach were still on, but when she looked through the palms toward the city, everything was black. She heard that Charles Taylor's troops were near the city. Soldiers were shooting out electrical transformers and cutting wires with bullets. Samuel Doe was still president and he was the target.

Dayou had also learned that the soldiers were looking for people of importance and anybody with money. Dayou and Mary were scared and had good reason to be. Since their dad was a tribal chief and a medicine man, the word was out that he would be killed. Mary's husband owned at least half of the garages in Monrovia, and she owned a restaurant, so they feared for their lives and the lives of their family.

A curfew had been set. Everybody had to be in their houses by five o'clock in the afternoon. A few days earlier, Dayou had been out to get water and the soldiers shot over her head.

* * *

A few days after fighting started in the city, Mary rushed to the house where Dayou was living to warn her of the danger of staying in Monrovia.

"We have to get out today," Mary said, gasping for breath. "Get your thing as fast as you can."

A short time later, Mary, her husband, her five-year-old daughter, her husband's two daughters by another wife and Dayou climbed into a covered truck. Each carried as much food as they could lift. Mary's husband paid the driver to take them to Bomi Hills, a town northeast of Monrovia, the shortest route home, away from the fighting. Once in Bomi Hills, they paid a lady to let them stay in her home. The lady and her family ate all the food Mary and her husband brought with them.

Several months later, the family decided to start walking home. They came to Bong Mines where iron ore had once been dug. The rebels had closed it and now used it as a checkpoint.

Soldiers, with their rifles drawn, watched the little group with cold eyes. Dayou huddled with the other children while Mary and her husband did the talking.

Suddenly, the landscape dimmed as clouds moved over the sun. Accusing her brother-in-law of being in President Doe's army, the soldiers said, "You have the mark of the boot on you."

"No, I have never been in the army. Not at any time," he responded.

The soldiers were members of a rebel group that wanted to overthrow President Doe. Mary and her husband didn't know if they were some of Charles Taylor's men or if they were with Prince Johnson, another insurgent.

The soldiers questioned Mary about her father. Hushing the other children, Dayou moved a little closer, straining to hear. Mary reported she had heard her father had been killed.

Dayou started shaking. She whispered to the other children not to talk. The sun came out warm and she noticed a snake lying in the weeds beside the road. She knew the minute he moved, the rifles would blast him into pieces. She silently willed him to be still.

The soldier in charge noticed Dayou's movement and asked, "Who are the children?"

Mary looked over at them as she replied, "The five-year-old is our daughter and the ten-year-old," pointing to Dayou, "is my half-sister, Layee."

Mary's husband put his arms around Charlotte, thirteen, and Mercy, seven, saying, "These are my daughters."

A guard spat out, "We know you have the mark of the boot on you. You're lying to us."

"I swear to you. I have never been in the army. I own some garages in Monrovia, and my wife has a restaurant. That's all." He wiped his forehead with his sleeve.

Dayou thought the reason they kept talking about the mark of the boot was because he was young and strong.

Behind the men, she saw a large mango tree with glossy leaves. She wondered how it survived the iron ore mining and now the deaths of people stopped at the checkpoint.

The wind shifted and she smelled a sick, sweet odor. The scent of decay lay heavy in the air. The temperature was about ninety with high humidity since it was almost the end of the rainy season. Dayou's mouth was like cotton, but she knew she couldn't ask for water. Suddenly, one of the young soldiers commanded Mary to stand with her legs wide apart. Dayou squeezed her eyes shut and covered her ears. When the soldier shot through Mary's legs, her husband cried. He was certain they would all be killed.

Dayou kept her eyes shut and her muscles tense waiting for the feel of a bullet. It never came. Instead, a soldier walked over to her and began to question her.

He nudged the rifle towards her as she opened her eyes. "Girl, you better tell the truth. What is your tribe?"

In fear, Dayou barely choked out, "Kpelle."

"How long has your brother-in-law been in the army?"

"He has never been in anybody's army. What he tells you is true. He works in his garages."

"How long have you been with them? Maybe he was in the army before you came."

"I was in Monrovia two years, since '88." Her heart was beating fast and she was sweating.

The soldier turned to look at his buddies and moved in their direction. They huddled to talk.

Dayou didn't want to hear their verdict. Instead, she concentrated on the deep pink of hibiscus in a planter nearby, wanting to disappear into the color.

The soldiers talked and argued for what seemed like an eternity to Dayou, maybe about what to do with the family. Their boss man was not there. In a few minutes, their missing leader returned from church, along with a young soldier. That a cold-blooded killer would go to church was beyond Dayou's understanding.

When the boss came up to his arguing soldiers, he demanded, "What are you doing with these people?"

33

"Getting ready to shoot them."

The boss studied their faces and said, "No, let them go."

Everybody was silent and the soldiers exchanged looks of disbelief. Dayou's shaking intensified while the soldiers continued to look at one another. From their reaction, Dayou sensed this had never happened before. People were killed at this checkpoint. When the family finally realized they were going to be spared, they whispered softly to one another, "This is our miracle Sunday."

* * *

In Carolinas' Medical, two men in green scrubs came into Dayou's room with a gurney to take her downstairs. They encouraged her to slide over onto it and she did. She tried to sound calm when she answered their questions. Once they were sure they had the right patient, they put a check next to Dayou's name on the paper attached to their clipboard and proceeded to whisk her out. Dayou grasped the metal railings more for emotional than physical support as they pushed her down the beige hall to the elevator.

6

GOING HOME

Bomi Hills

Breezes bring
a sick, sweet odor.
A scalp and dried fingers
hang on the wall.
Rumors of
my father's death sift in
through salty tears.

In the operating room, Dr. Rheindollar squeezed her hand and asked, "Dayou, how are you feeling? This won't take long and it will let us know what's going on with your liver."

Dayou gave the doctor a slight smile, closed her eyes and waited, her mind going back to Bomi Mines.

* * *

The young soldier, who had been to church, asked the family if they had a place to stay.

They said, "No," and, surprisingly, the boss man told them they could come to his house until his wife's family arrived from Monrovia.

35

Shadows lengthened as they walked down the street. Everyone was tired from fear and they were thirsty, but too tense to want food. There was a scalp with the skin curled below the hair and five fingers hanging like dried peppers on the wall in the room they were shown to in the boss man's house. The rebels liked to do weird things like that. Sometimes they put bones or other body parts on gates. Dayou shivered and cringed. She thought about the person who may have loved walking in the cool morning, eating rice and mangoes and smiling at little kids, someone like her in many ways, but someone who ended up a casualty in this senseless war. Not just a casualty, but one with body parts on display.

The family stayed at the boss man's house for one month. There was not much to eat at Bomi Mines – so many of them, so little food, but everybody shared what they had. Dayou was hungry most of the time. There wasn't much to do to divert her mind from food. Everywhere, they heard how whole families were being killed, children thrown into hundred-foot wells. Some afternoons, when the breeze blew in from the well, they smelled the sick, sweet odor of death. They believed with their whole hearts that God had saved them.

Dayou and Mary found another half-sister in town. One day a soldier made the sister and Mary watch the torture of a young boy the rebels believed had given information to the enemy. As they cut out his tongue, they said it was because he had talked too much. As they cut off his ears, they said he had listened to wrong things. Dayou's sisters tried to look away but the soldiers forced them to watch. The young women were horrified and told the gruesome story to their family when they got back to the house. Their parents were peaceful people who had taught them to hate violence, so this went against everything they knew and believed.

Four weeks after Miracle Sunday, the family started walking to Bong County where their parents lived. As they passed

through one of the villages, people informed them that Dayou
and Mary's father had been killed. In each village the same news
was told.

As they walked toward home, Dayou thought a lot about her
father and cried about never seeing him again. She had not lived
in his house since she had been in Monrovia but he was important
to her and she loved him.

As they came to the edge of a village near Totota, where Dayou's
father had a house on the street, she saw a familiar looking man in a
white African shirt. He was standing on the porch peering down the
road with his hand on his cheek as if he were puzzled. Was she
imagining things? The man shaded his eyes and leaned forward.

As they got closer, he ran down the street towards Dayou and
she started running towards him. It was her father. In his joy, he
grabbed her, lifted her into the air and swung her around. He said
that it was rumored that she had been killed and cut to pieces.
Dayou told him how they had thought he had been killed. They
laughed and looked lovingly at each other. After greeting the
others and hugging Mary, he took Dayou all around town to show
everybody that his daughter was still alive. He told her he had
been in hiding, but came home just a few days before. Dayou
would never forget the joy she felt that day. She had thought all
the good times were over.

The arrival of Dayou's group caused her father's other
children to have less to eat. But they shared their provisions,
which consisted of white potatoes and yams. Food was scarce
since her father had been hiding and had no chance to get money.

After a week in her dad's house, Dayou went to stay with her
Aunt Meatta, who had more food. Dayou had not had enough to
eat in over a year, so when she ate too much, she started throwing
up.

In 1991, Dayou decided to leave Totota and go to her mom's
place in the country. After speaking to two of her cousins at the

market, Dayou felt she could help her mother farm and take care of her baby brother. She would be thankful to see the sun come up, the wind moving in the trees and Grandmother Briggs smiling because her granddaughter was safe and home.

7

MOTHER FARMS

On the Farm

Mother chops, plants rice,
straightens
to rub her back.
I hand her the water jar,
droplets beading on the side.

Dayou's heart ached for home as she walked down the dusty road from Totota to her grandparents' place. Her mother, a strong, independent woman, had moved to the farm where she grew up when she left Dayou's father. Grandfather Briggs was dead, but Grandmother Briggs was there with her two sons, Joseph and Amos, and their four boys, who were all older than Dayou.

When the family heard Dayou was back from Monrovia, they went to see her at Aunt Meatta's. Dayou realized then how homesick she had been for them all, and she decided to go to her grandmother's house to live, a decision which upset Aunt Meatta.

The sun was hot and Dayou was glad to see through coconut palms and a big mango tree the outline of the concrete house with

39

its zinc roof. Her grandmother's little one-room house sat to the side, but Dayou did not see her in the yard. As she stepped through the front door of the big house, Dayou yelled, "Hey," but nobody answered. A breeze cooled her back as she walked through the hall looking into the six bedrooms. She heard a voice in the back. It was her grandmother talking to Dayou's baby brother as she laid brown cassava roots in the sun to dry. The baby was digging dirt with a spoon and dumping some into a small bowl.

Dayou stood quietly grinning until her grandmother turned. When she saw Dayou, her face lit up as she said, "Here's Layee. My goodness, child, I didn't know you were coming." She and the girl hugged while Dayou breathed in her good country smell. Dayou lifted her brother and held him on her lap as he watched her with big eyes before he decided to smile. As she squeezed him close, she thought he was the cutest baby she'd ever seen. He touched her face with his chubby hands, and she felt such an overpowering love that she knew she'd do anything to protect him.

Dayou and her grandmother sat in chairs on the patio, which was a low walled-in space with a dirt floor next to the house. They were silent, enjoying one another's presence.

"Wait here," Grandmother said. "I have something for you."

She groaned as she moved out of her chair. "My joints are hurtin' today. Let me get you some treats from my house."

She came back carrying a plate with dried fish, rice and two pieces of hard candy. Grandmother always had something hidden away for the children.

She asked about Aunt Meatta and the cousins. Dayou pinched the rice and fed some to the baby.

"Aunt Meatta has gone to work, and the others are playing around the house. I told them I was going to stay with you and Mother for a while. Is she in the field?"

"Yes. Amos and Joseph and their men's group helped her clear some more land. She and the women cooked for them, and last week, Joseph and the men used the wood they had cut to fence in the field. She carried some rice with her this morning, so I think she's ready to plant."

"I'll go find her," Dayou said. "Is she north of last year's field?"

"Yes. Take a water jar with you. She'll be thirsty working in this heat."

Dayou had eased the baby back down, handing him the spoon and bowl, which he banged on the ground.

She walked past Grandfather Briggs' garden, sliding her fingers in the wetness on the water jar and thinking of him. He'd been dead since she was a baby. Mother had said he was a cute man – tall, light-skinned and slender – who carried her all around on his shoulders showing her off. Dayou wished she could remember him and wished that he were still there. Nobody had taken good care of his garden. There were some bananas and pineapples, but weeds had taken over, standing tall as if they were some kind of plant people wanted.

She spotted her mother up ahead with the women in her work group, their hoes moving back and forth to the rhythm of the hymns they were singing from the Baptist church. They chopped the ground, sprinkled grains of rice and then chopped again to cover the seeds. Between songs, they laughed and talked. Dayou slowed down to watch her mother, who wore khaki pants, a long-sleeved, blue shirt and flip-flops. Her hands, larger than most women's, gripped the hoe handle and chopped the ground hard. She was no longer the chief's wife and was determined to feed her family.

Dayou saw her sister under the oak tree opening a bag of corn for the next section. She knew the other crops would be spinach, potatoes, peppers, onions, watermelons, cassava and pumpkins.

Mother straightened up, pressed her hand to her back and spotted her daughter. Dayou watched her smile spread.

She said, "Layee, I didn't know you were here. Oh, good, you brought some water."

They studied each other's faces before her mother tilted her head back to drink. Wiping her mouth on her sleeve, she said, "Layee, are you staying a while, long enough to grow a crop?"

"Yes, I want to."

"I'm asking because every time you come you start fussing with your sister after a couple of days and you get sassy with me. Then you run back to Meatta's. If you're staying, I'll give you a piece of this field and you can learn to farm."

"I'd like that. Can I plant some rice today?"

"Get busy."

* * *

About four in the afternoon, they straightened up, got the hoes and tied the tops of the seed bags together and started home. The women teased about who had done the most work and yelled goodbyes to each other. Dayou was exhausted when they got to the house and wanted to sit on the patio with a drink of water. The baby was asleep in Grandmother's house.

Mama was squatting to build a fire in the outdoor kitchen, feeding kindling in slowly when she asked Dayou to beat the cassava. Dayou told her she was tired, and she could get one of the other children to do that.

Her mom's voice got loud, "If you plan to eat, you'd better do what I say. You know the others are too short to do that, and the boys are still in the field. Besides, it's woman's work."

Sparks showered up from the dry wood. Dayou watched her mother's back and knew she'd better hush so she reached into the basket for a handful of the brown root and put some in the mortar

42

bowl. Mom was right. The stand for the bowl was as high as the table, and the younger children couldn't reach to beat it with the pestle, which always reminded her of a baseball bat.

The beating was one way to get over being mad. Mother was harder on her than she was on the others. If she didn't do all the work her mother laid out, she wouldn't let her eat. She and her mother hardly ever got along. Mom said punishment was for her own good, and someday she would appreciate it. Dayou thought it was just that mother-daughter thing.

The fire was burning, so Dayou took the ground cassava and dumped it into a pan with some water. The metal rack over the flames was about twelve inches high so she bent over to stir. Mother worked next to her cooking spinach and rice. She had put out a dish of palm oil with peppers for the rice.

When the cassava was the consistency of mashed potatoes, Dayou pushed it to the side so it would stay warm, saying, "The fufu's ready."

Dayou lifted a stack of plates to the table. The food odors mixed with wood smoke, and a day in the field made her hungry.

"Everything smells so good," she said.

"We'll have to wait for the neighbors. They're cooking chicken."

She knew how the meal would be. The men would sit at the table; the women would takes plates to chairs on the patio; the girls would go to the little hill in the side yard, and the boys would sit around the front of the house with their drinks on the steps. Dayou loved this about Africa. They shared their food so they wouldn't have to eat alone.

* * *

The next day her mother took some peppers out of Dayou's sister's rice and stuck them in Dayou's face trying to be funny.

43

Instead of laughing, Dayou got mad and slapped the peppers out of her mother's hand. Her mom jumped up to whip her, but Dayou ran so fast her mom couldn't catch her.

In the afternoon, Dayou and her cousin picked some pineapples from Grandfather's garden and took them into the village to sell.

Samuel, called Junior Boy, who was their favorite cousin, came by and asked for a pineapple. They told him, "You'll have to pay us seventy-five cents." He agreed, ate the pineapple and then wouldn't pay. Dayou's temper flared, and she slapped him on the back so hard he fell to the ground.

The next day Mom and Junior Boy grabbed Dayou and threw her down, and Junior Boy held her while Dayou's mom beat her with a shoe, a stick, anything she could get her hands on. Dayou knew she deserved a whipping, but she hated being held down, hated feeling she had no control, and she struggled hard to get loose.

Afterwards, Grandmother Briggs said, "Layee, I don't know why you are so bad. You are different from your mother or your daddy. Neither of them is as outspoken and strong-willed as you. Where does that stubborn streak come from? It sure is a mystery to me."

* * *

Dayou said her grandmother had been right because even if Dayou thought her life were in danger, she'd still say what she thought. She said she didn't want to die, but she would before she'd give over.

Now that she was sixteen, she understood that her mom had been trying to teach her the world was not an easy place, and she needed to learn to accept authority. In Africa, men were in charge, and women often had to use their wits and toughness to survive. Her mom had wanted to give Dayou the kind of strength she had, and Dayou said she hoped her mom was able to do that.

8

REBECCA

Leaving Home

*A truck carries us
to Nimba and Ivory Coast,
where cows wander the streets,
chickens run loose and
refugees ache for home.*

When I came into the hospital room on Saturday, Dayou was looking at her lunch tray. She lifted each lid and made a face when she smelled the pork and broccoli, but picked at the yams and ate the green Jell-O. I wanted her to try more, but she hated everything and wanted something from the Chinese Buffet on Eastway Drive.

This morning a test had been scheduled, so Dayou didn't get any food and instead had to drink a chalky mixture. Everything about Dayou's actions and attitude said she hoped this hospital stay would be over soon.

After having done some schoolwork, we watched *Fried Green Tomatoes* on TV. Both of us laughed and laughed when Twanda, played by Kathy Bates, repeatedly rammed the sassy girls' car and told them she was older and had more insurance.

Switching off the TV, I said, "I won't come tomorrow because it's Mothers' Day, and I'm meeting my children in Greensboro for dinner."

"That's okay. Miss Debra told me she will be by after church."

Mothers' Day was hard for Dayou. Her friends talked about gifts they had been considering for their moms and commercials on TV were full of suggestions.

Dayou said that sometimes she pretended her mother was here and planned the day. She imagined a menu for a special meal and a surprise gift wrapped in pink paper, tied with white ribbons. She said she would not let her mom do any work on that Sunday. She'd tell her she loved her. It had been six years since she last saw her mother.

* * *

In 1991, Dayou's uncle came to her mother's farm and said Aunt Meatta wanted her to come to her house in Totota. He said she wanted Dayou to go to Ivory Coast with a lady named Rebecca Tucker, who rented a booth in a warehouse and sold food. Rebecca needed someone who could help her with the business. Aunt Meatta said Dayou was a good worker and would be the best one to go. Dayou never had a say in the decision.

She told her family goodbye, kissed her baby brother and started walking to Totota. Outside her father's house, she paused and looked up at the door for a long time. She didn't think he was there so she kept walking. Later, she asked herself why she didn't stop and leave him a message.

Leaving Liberia had not bothered Dayou because she had spent most of her life living with different relatives – sometimes with Aunt Meatta, or in Monrovia with her half-sister. That's how it was over there. Liberians believed children were too precious to be raised by only two people. Although this would be

48

her first time to leave the country, Dayou thought she could always come back home. To her, this was just another day in her young life.

After she got to Aunt Meatta's, they talked about the trip, then climbed into a taxi, but it was not really a taxi – a bus, but not a bus. It was more like a truck, but the back was covered and there were seats along each side. Rebecca also took her niece Nancy, who was seven years old and had always lived with her. They rode all day and Dayou got car sick and threw up. That night they slept in Nimba, a county bordering Ivory Coast. Some people who had known Rebecca gave them rice for supper and a place to sleep. The next day they arrived in Danane, Ivory Coast.

Dayou, Rebecca, and Nancy lived in an apartment with Rebecca's husband, James Tucker. In the mornings, the two girls attended a small school which was behind their apartment. The teachers spoke English even though French was the language of Ivory Coast. Dayou was eleven but since she had been to school very little, she was placed in first grade. They sang "Twinkle, Twinkle," learned the ABCs and numbers. School was out every day at twelve o'clock.

Cows wandered down the streets and chickens ran loose, too. The town was very dirty. The terrible time was when it rained and chicken and cow manure swirled around their feet.

There were lots of Liberians in the country. The government of Ivory Coast had allowed them to come in, but they didn't give money or any help to the refugees. The Tuckers, Nancy and Dayou had been waiting to get a visa to the U.S. James, who Dayou called her uncle, had worked for the Voice of America in Monrovia. Since it was an American organization, he said they would take care of them.

Rebecca was a very beautiful woman with soft waves in her hair and bright, red lipstick. She was an excellent cook. She and Dayou prepared food in the apartment and sold it in the mornings and in the late afternoons. There were pans of fu-fu, rice with sauce, okra and beans.

Men getting off work in the factory stopped to buy from them. They said the food was delicious, better than they were used to eating.

The food Dayou cooked was something like doughnuts, sweet bread that she fried. She made some of these in the apartment and wrapped them in foil. As soon as she got to the warehouse booth, customers were lined up to buy them. She began frying more, and as each one was lifted out of the pan, customers would say, "That's mine," and another one claimed the next one until they were all gone. People in Ivory Coast were crazy about those sweets.

She sold her food so quickly that other folks in the warehouse said she was a witch, that she cast a spell on customers that made them want her sweets more than what was offered in other booths. Dayou just laughed and cooked faster.

Her job was to stay in the booth and sell. She was expected to help every day when school was out while Nancy stayed home. Dayou worked so much that the landlady at their apartment got angry because she saw that Nancy was allowed to play, but Dayou was not.

Sometimes Nancy ate some of the food that wasn't hers. For instance, she might eat the meat out of James' soup, and, if Dayou didn't give her money, she'd say Dayou had done it and get Dayou in trouble.

One day Rebecca left and the girls didn't known where she was. They found food she had cooked for them, but they didn't know when they'd see her again. After a few days, Rebecca returned.

Soon Dayou got yellow jaundice and was so sick she had trouble seeing. She told Rebecca about the medicine her mother had used to make her better, the one made from the second skin of a tree, but Rebecca didn't do anything about it. Dayou had to go out to get water when she could hardly see enough to walk. She carried a bucket to the well and the metal handle cut into her hand as she struggled back to the apartment. One day a Frenchman, a friend of Rebecca's, gave Dayou some medicine and she finally felt better.

She knew when she was sick and Rebecca wouldn't help her that Rebecca was very different from Dayou's mother or her aunt. Rebecca made Dayou work like a slave.

After they received letters saying they would get visas to the U.S., Dayou saw her cousin's wife on the street. Dayou told her they were leaving, and her cousin's wife said, "Let me take your picture and I'll send it to your mother." Rebecca said, "No, you can't do that."

Dayou didn't know why Rebecca didn't want her mother to have that picture. She thought about it often but never understood.

One night, she overheard Rebecca and James talking. Rebecca wanted to take Nancy and Dayou back to Liberia, but James said, "No, I want them to go with us. We shouldn't leave them in Liberia. There's heavy fighting in places. They might be killed."

They spent a year and a half in Danane and then in June of 1993, they all got on a bus to go to Abidjan to apply for passports in preparation for leaving the country. Rebecca warned Dayou not to eat much because she remembered how she got sick riding. Dayou was careful but knew she was going to throw up anyway. James took off his little round, black African hat and gave it to her to throw up in. It was all they had.

Rebecca got so mad and she started yelling, "I told you not to eat. You greedy self!" James told Rebecca to leave Dayou alone, that she couldn't help being sick.

They stayed for a week in Abidjan in a hotel. The town was cleaner and much prettier than Danane.

When they got on the plane, Dayou was afraid to eat, so James ate his meal and Dayou's.

Dayou was so excited about going to the U.S. A long time ago, her mother's youngest sister had gone to the States after finishing high school and had never come back. She had the most education of anyone in the family. Dayou hoped to find her, but all she'd ever seen was a picture sent in a brown envelope. She tried to remember her face. The photograph was at Aunt Meatta's house in Totota.

As they flew to Brussels and then to New York, Dayou didn't think she'd go home to live with her family again. Since her aunt didn't come back, she doubted she would. She ached to see her baby brother and asked herself why she hadn't told her father goodbye.

9

ARRIVING

America

It's the same –
earth, trees, sky –
like Africa.
People walk,
feet touching the ground.

Dayou returned to school the day after she was released from the hospital. She worried about how she would handle the long hours.

When I called, she said, "I have stomach pains all day and the diarrhea never lets up. I went to sleep in class. People asked about my yellow eyes, and I didn't have a good answer for them."

Dayou wondered if she would be able to finish ninth grade. I wondered if she could start tenth in the fall. A day at school was so close to being too much. How would she feel by the end of the summer?

As a former middle school teacher, I knew that going to the next grade at the beginning of a school year was like crossing a bridge to another level of your life. Dayou saw the new clothes, book bags and schedules as a celebration of moving on. All of this weighed her down.

Dayou was glad for school to be over. Some days she had been so sick she'd called Debra to come get her. She hated feeling so bad but during the summer she could stay home and rest, even though being in the apartment all day was boring. She slept late, read or watched TV and talked on the phone. She always had diarrhea and her stomach hurt. Because of the liver disease, her abdomen was swelling, so it was hard to find clothes that were comfortable. Her eyes stayed yellow. Sometimes she would go into her room, close the door and cry.

Her uncle heard her sobs and said, "Please don't cry. You'll be all right." I know he felt helpless.

One night Dayou's friend Lady knocked on the door and didn't get an answer. She was scared so she went to a phone and called. Dayou thought she must have passed out because she hadn't heard the knock. Lady was worried and stayed with Dayou as much as she could.

Dayou tried to do a few things with the youth at church. I picked her up on Wednesday afternoons and we worked on math and English, but some days she was too sick and put her head down on the table in the church library.

During the long days in the apartment she thought about home. She said she was mad about being sick. She wasn't afraid to die but she didn't want it to be in a strange country. She wanted to be with family, especially her mother. She said she needed to be with people who could look at her and tell that she was not doing well. Her father, mother, brothers and sisters would know by watching her eyes. When she was the sickest, her eyes were always red or yellow.

If it was her time to go, she wanted them to stand around her bed and watch her die. She wanted to be able to tell them all the things she never got to say like, "If I caused you any pain, I'm sorry. I love you, and even after I'm gone and not here in flesh, I'll always be around you in spirit."

She didn't want to die in this country and if she did, she didn't want to be buried here. She was afraid nobody would send her body home. She wanted to be buried with her brothers and sisters.

She'd been here almost four years, away from home six. She remembered her first sight of the U.S.

* * *

They landed at JFK in New York but Dayou didn't know where they were. She thought it might be another African country. Someone from Catholic Social Services had met them in Brussels, and someone else from that group met them in New York. A piece of their luggage was missing, so they decided to stay overnight. The social worker said he would take them to a hotel.

As they stepped out of the airport and stood on the sidewalk, cars rushed by. There were people everywhere. Dayou tried to figure out if this really was America. She thought things would be different here until she saw the earth, trees, sky and people who walked around with their feet touching the ground. There were no robots to do everything for you. She didn't even look up at the tall buildings.

They were tired when they got to the hotel, so James ordered meatballs and macaroni from room service. The Tuckers laughed about the huge meatballs, but, despite their hunger, none of them could eat because they were so exhausted. They took showers and fell into bed.

The next day their luggage arrived, so they returned to the airport and flew to Charlotte, North Carolina. Martha Ajavon met the plane. She was from Liberia and held the baby of another Liberian refugee, Joseph Dennis. The baby's name was Willis. Rebecca and James knew Martha in Ivory Coast. She was a tall, imposing woman with strong features who walked with a regal bearing like an African queen. Martha's husband had been killed by the rebels.

Another person at the airport was Will Coley from the Refugee Office of Catholic Social Services. Dayou thought he was so nice. The two of them talked as if they had met before.

James tried, in vain, to claim their now missing luggage before Martha and Will drove them to the place where they would live. The apartment, which Martha and Will had furnished, had a kitchen, living room, two bedrooms and a bathroom. Martha had done a lot of work to get everything ready for the travelers and had even cooked an African meal with soup, dry rice with okra and shrimp.

This was not the first time Dayou had watched programs on TV because her sister and aunt in Monrovia each had one. But here they watched a lot because the family had heard how dangerous it was in America, and they were afraid to go outside. People from home, who had lived here for a while and gone back, had told them that you weren't supposed to open the door until you looked through a little glass and recognized the visitor. They said folks had been shot in the streets. At home people had been killed in war, but Dayou didn't know if she could ever feel safe in a place where shootings occurred daily.

It was June and the air conditioning made them cold. They were freezing all the time, but they didn't know how to change the temperature, and they stayed in the apartment because of their fear.

After two weeks, Martha came and asked, "Why are you staying in the house? I can't believe you haven't been out since I left." After listening to Dayou and her family's reasons, Martha

56

laughed and told them it was safe to leave the apartment, and she showed them how to turn the thermostat up.

A fifteen-year-old girl from Liberia was with Martha. Her name was Lady Dennis. Dayou had seen her in Ivory Coast but had not met her. They told the Tuckers about a day camp for refugee children at Resurrection Lutheran Church, only a few blocks away. Dayou was thirteen and Nancy eight. Martha said they could both go and that Lady's brother Lafayette, who was eight, would also be there.

The camp was fun with Bible studies and games. The children were from different countries like Vietnam, Laos, plus African countries other than Liberia. This time was nice for Dayou because she began a friendship with Lady.

Will Coly visited them regularly to find out what was needed. He took them to get shots, brought books and dolls and drove them to Crisis Assistance Ministry to get clothes. Dayou's first book was *Curious George* and then Dr. Seuss. The most exciting thing Will did was to take them to Carowinds.

When the bus left with about ten people from the day camp, Dayou wondered what Carowinds would be like. Will explained it was a theme park with rides, but that really didn't mean much to her.

After they got in the gate, Dayou, Lady, Vinnie, an Asian girl and Martha's son Austin walked around together. They bought pretzels and sweets and then headed for the rides.

Dayou screamed all the way through the ride on the Oaken Bucket as it whirled so fast they were pushed back against the wall and hung there. The second one was the roller coaster. Dayou sat with Austin, buckled her seat belt, and when they started down the steep grade screamed, "I want my mommy! I'm going to die!" She grabbed Austin around the neck and almost choked him. The more frightened she was, the harder she squeezed.

57

When they got off, Lady and Vinnie wanted to ride again. Austin, rubbing his neck, said, "We'll wait because I never intend to get on a roller coaster with Dayou again."

They met the others at noon. Austin's older brother Isaac had fixed their lunch, which was sandwiches made with soft-cooked eggs, cheese and tomatoes. It looked gooey and awful, but Dayou had to admit it tasted pretty good.

At four in the afternoon, they went to the bus to head home after an exciting, scary and wonderful day. They laughed, told each other their adventures and slowly grew quiet. They were half asleep before the bus squeaked to a stop.

10

SCHOOL IN AMERICA

School

My teacher dances
with me on Black History Day.
I cheer for the team
in a green uniform,
struggle to catch up.

In late summer, Will took Dayou, Nancy and Rebecca to Crown Point Elementary so the girls could register. It was a new school. Everything looked bright, and the floors were shiny. On the first day, Rebecca went to the bus stop with the girls. Dayou was not exactly scared, but she wondered what it would be like. She had only been to kindergarten and first grade. In Liberia you were placed according to your skills regardless of your age, but here she would be in sixth grade with twelve-year-olds.

Ms. Young was her English teacher, Ms. Kiss, her math teacher. On the playground, she sat and watched other kids. Ms. Johnson, a teacher's assistant, helped her read and called out her spelling words. While the others did reading, Ms. Johnson took Dayou into another room. She was so kind; in fact, for Dayou, she was the best part of sixth grade. During Black History celebration, Ms. Young and Dayou danced together.

Two months after school started, the teachers decided to put Dayou in ESL (English as a Second Language) class. English was her first language, along with Kpelle, but in Liberia, her family used a type of pigeon English that made speaking and understanding here difficult.

Every day after lunch, she went to the ESL classroom for about thirty minutes.

She was chosen to be in a school play, which was about going to Russia. Dayou was so pleased to have her first chance to act, and she loved it.

Having the year end was the worst thing about sixth grade. Because she didn't want to leave Ms. Johnson, Dayou cried all the way home on the bus. School was now a shining part of her life, unlike the way it had been in Totota. Here, every day was a struggle to try to learn so much she had missed. But, as a young girl away from her family, she treasured the warm relationships with teachers.

The ESL teacher took her to visit three middle schools so she could decide where she wanted to go the next year. At Hawthorne, a girl threatened to beat her up so that one was out. Another school had dirty bathrooms and too many pregnant girls. They had been doing their hair in the cafeteria. This did not appeal to Dayou. She chose Piedmont Open Middle School. When she began in the fall, she found that most of the kids were in little groups. One asked her to join, and when she refused, they called her African Boodie and said she smelled like fish.

All her friends at Piedmont were from other countries. An adult friend, Ms. Casandra Drakeford, was secretary in the guidance office. Dayou became her assistant and Ms.Drakeford helped her out any way she could. If someone threatened Dayou, she told Ms. Drakeford, and Ms. Drakeford made sure Dayou was safe. One day she even went to Dayou's apartment and styled Dayou's hair.

Mr. Dula, her English teacher, had dreadlocks and wore a beard. Dayou was afraid of him at first, but soon learned that he was a very nice teacher.

Her social studies teacher, Mr. Lydden, let her call him at home if she had questions or needed help preparing for a test.

During the seventh grade, there was trouble between James and Rebecca, and Rebecca left. She took Nancy and asked if Dayou wanted to come with them. Dayou said, No, she'd stay with her uncle.

Rebecca and Nancy then moved to an apartment about half a mile away. Dayou's uncle was good to her. He did the housework and let her work on her lessons.

In the eighth grade, she tried out for cheerleader, which required taking forms around for her teachers to sign. To be selected, a student had to have a positive attitude and good grades. Dayou was on the "B" Honor Roll. She and her friend Kathy, who waited with her at the bus stop, were both chosen. Ms. Drakeford was the sponsor for the cheerleaders, and Dayou felt she may have been the one who gave her this chance.

On the day before a pep rally, she knew her nose was starting to bleed. It sounded crazy to other people but Dayou could smell the blood before anyone could see it. The P.E. teacher, principal, assistant principal and counselor tried to help her in the bathroom. She had to tell them she had hepatitis, and they must be careful not to touch the blood. It kept gushing so they called the ambulance. The EMT's were finally able to stop the bleeding, but she was not allowed to take part in the pep rally.

* * *

In the spring, Dayou was recommended by her counselor to receive the Youth Recognition Award from the Charlotte City Council. She had to write a paper about her life, coming to this

61

country and how she stayed positive. She and several other students were given the award by Mayor Pat McCrory before the Charlotte City Council. Lady, her dad, Joseph Dennis, her brothers and Dayou's friends Jay and Christy Godwin were present. Dayou was especially excited when the mayor presented her with the certificate. She felt honored to be recognized by him.

That night she felt a mixture of emotions. Running through it all was the wish that her family could be there to cheer for her and share her pride.

At the end of eighth grade, there was a graduation. Ms. Drakeford was the only one who came to see her walk across the stage. Dayou's nose started bleeding again, but she didn't tell anyone since it stopped before the ceremony began. Dayou cried as she walked over to get her certificate. She had been happy at Piedmont, but this was another ending which heralded another move. She so wanted her life to be stable, to stay at Piedmont among those who were familiar to her and with whom she felt comfortable.

Dayou with James Tucker when she was honored by the mayor of Charlotte.

11

ON TO HIGH SCHOOL

West Charlotte High

Strange faces,
bells ringing,
rushing to classes.
One shiny hope:
a teacher who asks me
to speak Kpelle.

Dayou's ninth grade class was the first to go to senior high. The school system wanted to make this move earlier but there had been no space in the senior high buildings. It was a new experience for fourteen-year-olds to be in high school, so some of the teachers went with them.

Starting school was not too hard for Dayou because when the schedule came out, Lady took her to West Charlotte High and showed her where each class would be. Then, on the first day, Lady came each time the bell rang and walked with Dayou to make certain she didn't get lost.

Ms. Drakeford was in the guidance office. Mr. David Butler and his friend Mr. Don Daniel had also transferred from Piedmont. Dayou was so glad to see their faces in all the scary, newness of a big school.

Mr. Butler was her math teacher. She had not been in his class in middle school, but they knew each other. He was so good with the students, and they all loved him. He made corny jokes, and when the students acted up, he quoted scripture like, "When I was a child, I spoke as a child… but when I become a man, I put away childish things." Other days he started class with a different quote from the Bible. He went over the math problems and helped students work them correctly.

Dayou looked forward to seeing him every morning. When she came down the hall, she always spotted his tall, slender profile leaning against the door. He had a mustache and a warm smile. He said "Hello, Dayou. Say something to me in Kpelle." She never used her native dialect with him. She didn't know why, except she was beginning to lose it since she seldom spoke it.

Six months into the year, everyone came to school on what seemed to be an ordinary morning. It was January 7th, and they learned that Mr. Butler's house had caught fire during the night. He had put his wife, his fourteen-year-old daughter and six-year-old son out the front window and, while they stood waiting, told them he would go out the back. The window had been too small for him to crawl through. The dead bolt was on the back door and he must have been overcome by smoke because the firemen found his body inside.

A dark gloom settled over the whole school with teachers and students crying. Nobody could think of anything else. Dayou could hardly bear to be in his classroom without him. The emptiness swallowed her. She thought about his friend, Mr. Daniel, and knew he was taking this so hard. He had left school when he heard the news.

Counselors talked to students who were upset. Dayou cried, but did not want to see a counselor. Lady sat with her.

* * *

At the funeral home she waited in line, wiping tears and wondering how Mr. Butler would look in the casket. Her turn came, and she walked over to see his body. He was a light-skinned African-American and had a lot of make-up on, but he didn't look dead. He just looked like Mr. Butler. He was dressed up in a suit and tie. At school he had always worn regular clothes, like plaid shirts and khaki pants. She couldn't believe he was dead. It was as if he'd gone someplace else.

She leaned over the satiny side and whispered in Kpelle, "I'm going to miss you. You were a good teacher. I'm sorry I never told you in my language." She stood by the casket touching the soft edge, choked by tears.

Then she turned and slowly moved past the long line of mourners, speaking only to students and teachers she knew. Outside, she shivered and pulled her coat tight in the cold January air.

It was unreal that she would not greet Mr. Butler at the door Monday morning or wait to ask for help on a homework problem or groan at one of his silly jokes or hear him say, "Please, Dayou, speak to me in Kpelle." The sign would still be under the clock in his room, "Time passes. Will you?"

* * *

Days dragged on, and there was talk about how to honor him. Donations were made to his family, who no longer had a husband, a father or a home. Weeks later the school planted a tree in his memory and his wife came for the ceremony.

Finally, the decision was made to name the new high school that was being built, David Butler High. Dayou liked this. He had not been a famous person, but someone who had spent his life giving to others, which she thought was more important than being famous. She hoped the students who would go there would find out what he was like.

* * *

A bright spot at West Charlotte was ROTC. Dayou liked the discipline and order and was proud to wear the uniform every Wednesday. She and Colonel Love got along. He called her "Tucker," and sometimes he asked her to do special jobs for him. He had retired from the military as a lieutenant colonel and enjoyed helping students take pride in their accomplishments. He told people Dayou was his daughter and she always felt he saw her as a good person, someone who could achieve, which encouraged her.

Other ROTC officers who were important in her life were Master Sergeant Smith, who called her "Dayou" and also acted like a father to her and Sergeant Major Harris, who talked to her a lot. He said, "You have potential, Miss Tucker. You are a strong, independent woman."

***

In February, Dayou told me about the ROTC dance coming up at the Hilton and said she needed a dress. I brought her one of my daughter's dresses, and it fit well except it was too long. Tamara was five-seven and Dayou was five-two. It was a nice shade of royal blue and made in a tailored style which suited her figure. Dayou liked the way it looked on her. Nell Mullis, a friend at church, hemmed it and sewed ribbons on the back to keep the straps from slipping off her shoulders and even gave her a strapless bra to wear with it. I loaned her my white coat.

On the day of the dance, Debra took Dayou to get her hair done. When she was dressed and ready to go, she looked in the mirror and wished her mother could see her. She knew she'd have said, "Layee, you look pretty," and she would have given her and Lady each a hug before they left.

When they arrived at the dance, they got in line to have their pictures taken. Dayou hoped there would be a time when she could find out if her family was okay and send them a picture of herself in the long, blue dress.

Dayou dressed for the ROTC dance.

12

SEARCHING FOR DAYOU'S FAMILY

Jesse Karnley

A Liberian man knows my uncle,
moves the pen to write
my parents' names.
The words help me
leap over the ocean.

On a Wednesday in July, I asked Dayou to be at church to hear our guest speaker, Jesse Karnley, who was from Liberia. He had been in the cabinet of Samuel Doe, Liberia's former president.

Everybody crowded into the Fellowship Hall, including the teenagers and children. Mr. Karnley began by telling us that when he was a boy walking down a dusty road in the bush with his mother, a missionary had stopped to talk to them. During the conversation, the missionary had recognized that Jesse appeared to be a quick learner and had suggested to his mother that he be allowed to live in the mission compound where he could attend school. She agreed and a whole new world opened to him. He

69

began reading and absorbing everything at a rapid pace. He was able to go to college. Rev. Karnley went on to say that he had worked as a TV journalist and had been described as the Walter Kronkite of Monrovia, but that because he had served with President Doe, he had become a wanted man. He was captured by Charles Taylor's rebel troops and sent before a firing squad. He described the morning when he walked out with his hands tied behind his back, quoting scripture. Miraculously, there had been a last minute change in orders, and his life had been spared.

"I tried to stay on in Monrovia," he said, "where by this time I was the pastor of a church. The fighting became so intense that I escaped on a ship and came to Charlotte seeking political asylum."

As I listened to him tell about his life, I realized that he knew many people in Liberia. He said his daughter was still working in Monrovia.

Lois Bumpus and I had tried to locate Dayou's family. Dayou wanted to know if they survived the war. We were aware of the seriousness of her illness and felt we might need to be in touch with them.

Because of Dayou's limited schooling before she left home, and because her father had a tribal name, we could not tell by her pronunciation how it would be spelled. What Dayou told us sounded like she was saying, *Yellow Cola.*

I found on the internet that a short-wave radio tower had been built in Totota a few months earlier. I thought perhaps missionaries or friends, who had short wave access, could begin trying to make contact for us if we had a close-to-accurate spelling. Lois and I were dealing with the first situation in our lives where we could not find the spelling of names we needed.

After the service, I talked with Reverend Karnley, who was a nice looking gentleman with brown skin and short, graying hair. I asked if he could meet with Dayou, Lois and me and give us some help. I pulled out folding metal chairs, and the four of us sat down at a banquet-sized table with a fake wood top. I placed paper and pen near his hand and hoped there would be something to write.

I explained our problem. He began to question Dayou about her parents.

She said, "My dad is a chief in Bong County and his last name is Kolo."

"I know of him. He is Yerkorer Kolo." He picked up the pen and wrote the words as he spoke.

I glanced at Dayou. Her smile started slowly and then spread to her whole face as she looked at Lois and me. At the same time I heard an "Oh" from Lois and I felt excitement building as Rev. Karnley asked, "How about your mother?"

"Her maiden name is Briggs, first name is something like Sangy."

As we watched, his brown hand moved the pen again. He wrote "Sangay Briggs."

"Does your mother have a brother who lives in Monrovia?"

"Yes, she does."

"I know the exact house he lives in. Yes, I most certainly do."

Dayou and Rev. Karnley began talking about streets and certain locations they both knew well, and they were laughing together.

My eyes stayed on the paper tracing the letters mentally as if I were afraid they'd be lost again. We sat on either side of Rev. Karnley. There was something almost mystical about this man who had escaped death and walked into our lives bringing words we needed.

When Dayou had gone to school in Ivory Coast, the teacher had misunderstood her name and written *Dayou* instead of *Layee*. From that time on her name had been officially changed. Now, we had another piece of the puzzle – *Layee Kolo*.

I asked about radio in Monrovia. Rev. Karnley told us that everybody listened to BBC and that each day there were lists read of people trying to locate family and friends. These announcements required payment, but he knew his daughter could get the information and the money to the station. I asked about the availability of electricity. He shared that residents of Bong County used battery-powered radios, and, if her parents missed the announcement, he was certain someone else could get word to them. We gave him forty dollars to wire to his daughter.

I walked to the car holding the piece of paper with names on it. I thought about the importance of the written word and what a wall we ran into without it. The kids Dayou knew were able to spell their parents' names. Now she could, too.

* * *

The next week Lois went to Washington, D.C. to visit her son. She called to say she had contacted the Liberian Embassy with the names she had. The man who answered the phone did not seemed interested in helping in any way. Lois didn't know if he was suspicious of her motives, but, regardless, he wouldn't give any information. She asked about Dayou's family and also about the mother of Lady Dennis.

The man told Lois that the girls would have to come to Washington. Lois explained that they were in high school and did not have the money to come. His final answer was that there was no way he could help.

Meanwhile, I called people I knew who had worked with short wave radio. Frances Nakamura, who was retired from WSOC-TV, said that because of the time difference, it would be difficult to be on the air when someone from Totota happened to be on. But he was willing to try, and he would also get some friends to help.

Brenda Deese, from another church, heard about our problem and thought she had some contacts that could help. She had visited some missionaries in Africa and called one in Ivory Coast, giving him the names. He promised to try to reach Dayou's parents on the radio, and if he were unsuccessful, he would ask among the refugees for someone who had recently come from Bong County. While we were waiting, Brenda also sent a letter through the Red Cross.

In a few days, Dayou came running down the walkway at church. Her face was beaming and I knew something big had happened.

"Mrs. Noell! Mrs. Noell! My family is safe. Nobody was killed in the war. I'm so happy."

"That's wonderful, Dayou." I reached out to hug her. "How did you find out?"

"Mrs. Deese, the missionary, called, went on the short wave radio and picked up a man in Totota. He asked him if he knew anyone in the family of Layee Kolo, the daughter of Yerkorer Kolo."

"He said, 'I certainly do. Her half-brother Jackson lives next-door to me. He said that all the family escaped the war. The missionary gave him my phone number, and asked him to have my brother call. I can't wait to talk to him. Can you believe this? I'm going to be able to talk to my family!"

This was in the miracle category. There was very little mail getting into Totota and no phone lines. I had anticipated months of trying to make a radio contact. It was almost unbelievable that none of her family had been lost in the war, unbelievable that her brother lived next-door to the radio operator. Dayou and I smiled and smiled as we thought about what had happened.

She was at school the first time her brother tried to call. Dayou hated missing his call, but waited for another contact. A few days later, she answered the phone and a voice with the accent from home said, "This is Jackson." She was afraid someone might be trying to trick her, so she asked him to say her mother's name and those of her brother and sisters. She also asked the name of his sister and the age of her child. After she was satisfied that he was who he said he was, she sighed heavily, and they began exchanging news.

Jackson talked about serving in Charles Taylor's army and said he was using the phone in Taylor's headquarters. Dayou told him about high school, friends and her youth group at church.

He told her the family had no money and asked if she could send some. She explained that she was a full-time student and had little opportunity to earn any.

He said, "The man who told me where you are used to live in the U.S. He said everyone there can get money. When he was in the states, he was only fourteen, but he drove a cab and had worked at other jobs. Please find a way to work and send something to us. There are no jobs here."

After goodbyes and the click of the broken connection, Dayou heard the drone of the dial tone. She held the phone, rubbing the edge with her fingers before placing it back in the cradle. She was surprised to see her hand shaking.

13

THE DOCTOR DECIDES

July 10, 1997

Peter, my elder brother, writes,
"We are praying God
that she will be well."
He signs,
"Nylia Kolo – Father
Sangay Kolo – Mother
Miata Briggs – Aunt"

Dayou thought September was one of the hardest months of her life. She started back to school even though she was sick. One day she came home and her stomach was hurting so much she lay down on the floor. Her friend Sheryl called, and Dayou started crying, so Sheryl called her mother Leslie, who left work and took Dayou to Carolinas' Medical. About midnight they went home to Leslie's house where Dayou swallowed the white pills they had given her at the hospital. She was thirsty, eating ice constantly. During the night, she got so sick she knocked on Leslie's door, and before her friend's mother could open it, Dayou saw whirling black and collapsed to the floor. Leslie called 911, and the paramedics took Dayou back to the hospital. Her plasma was low.

During September, Dayou was home a few days. Then Debra took her back to the hospital. Dayou had big knots on her hands and all over her body. They itched so badly she was miserable. The transplant team gave her a liquid medicine.

One day she woke up in the hospital. Her last memory had been of being with Rebecca, James' ex-wife. Debra told her she had gotten so sick they had to rush her to the emergency room. Dayou had tried to hit the nurse who put in her IV. She looked down and saw her hands tied to the bed. Dayou was given some yellow, slick medicine, which made her shiver as it went down. She couldn't figure out what had made her act so crazy.

* * *

In early October, Dr. Rheinhollar asked Dale Harlan, Debra Hayes, James Tucker and me to come to Carolinas' Medical for a conference. We expected to hear that Dayou was on the transplant list.

Dr. Rheindollar sat midway down at a conference table. He had an oval face, blue eyes and a light mole on his right cheek. His head was bald in front, with gray hair cut very short around the back. His expression was pleasant, with an easy smile. He looked slowly around the room as he studied each face.

"Some of you I know," he said. "Others I have not met. Please introduce yourselves, and, as you do, tell me your connection with Dayou."

James, who was in his mid-sixties, explained that he was Dayou's uncle and that he had escaped war in Liberia and now worked two jobs in Charlotte. His skin was the deep brown of West Africa, his frame small and furrows creased his face. He had a patient weariness that spoke of having endured hard times.

Debra Hayes, an articulate, self-confident woman, no stranger herself to adversity, was the other black at the table. She wore a white pants suit and gold earrings. Debra had a history of surviving. She had once driven a cab in New York at night while her young children slept on the front seat. She was on staff at Briar Creek Road Baptist Church and now worked with the poor, especially single mothers who needed a hand up.

Next to Debra, sat Dale Harlan, who explained that he was pastor at Briar Creek Road Baptist, where Dayou was a member. He shared that his dream was to have an international congregation and that he was willing to go the second mile. His face shone with enthusiasm and concern.

I sat at the end of the table and told Dr. Rheindollar that I had tutored Dayou for the past two years. I mentioned her joy at making the "B" honor roll last year and that she had been honored by the Charlotte City Council as a student who had a positive attitude in the face of a difficult situation.

Also present were Suzanne, a transplant nurse, and Cheree, a hospital social worker.

After the introductions, Dale and Debra talked about the support Dayou had at the church, mentioning that a number of people had volunteered to help any way they could.

Cheree expressed her concern that without family here, Dayou did not have enough support for the after-care required with a transplant.

Debra shook her head. "Our people will do whatever is necessary. I know a care team can be organized, and we'll see to it that her needs are met."

Dr. Rheindollar began, "I have studied Dayou's case carefully. She has an unusual situation because she has hepatitis, B and D." He paused, fingered his pen as we studied his face searching for clues. He wrote "B" and "D" on his notepad and drew a box around the letters.

"If we do surgery, I think the disease will return with more vengeance."

James shifted and his chair creaked. A horn blew outside the window.

Dr. Rheindollar paused, "A transplant would not work with her diagnosis, so I won't put her on the waiting list." He rubbed his forehead between his eyes, showing the anguish that came with this pronouncement.

I felt as if someone had hit me in the chest. It was hard to breathe. Everyone was silent with only the hum of the air conditioning breaking into the quiet.

The doctor looked around the table at each of us and said, "I know this is hard for you to hear. All of you are involved in her life."

We were in shock. All of us, except perhaps the hospital staff, had come expecting a different outcome. The quiet was almost suffocating since I knew Dayou was counting on a transplant as her last hope as she waited in her hospital room. I couldn't bear to think about the moment she heard this news. She was so sick, already in liver failure, but certain we'd return assuring her she was going to make it with the transplant. I began to think about life without her.

Wednesdays would be the worst because that had been our day together. I always had Dayou on my mind as I got material off the internet for her projects and spent time thinking about other sources. Then there were Sundays. At the end of service, Dayou would come over to hug me and we'd talk about the coming week. Without her, there would be an empty hole in my life. I thought going to church might be hard.

"How long does she have?" I asked, my raspy voice breaking the heavy silence in the room.

"Maybe a few weeks. At the most, a month or two," replied Dr. Rheindollar.

Trying to control my voice, I asked, "What can we do for her now?"

We began to talk about using a three-person team to go to her apartment in shifts. We discussed the danger of infection and the need for hepatitis shots for each caregiver.

"What will the end be like?" asked Debra.

"One possibility is that she will bleed to death."

This was a second blow. I couldn't even begin to imagine the horror of that kind of death for her.

Dr. Rheindollar continued, "You have already seen episodes of nose bleeds. Soon, the clotting action of the blood will be destroyed. These episodes will be very difficult for you to handle in the home. If possible, hospice will come in to help, but they don't stay all day."

I could feel my heart beating when I said, "Dayou knows we're meeting, and she's waiting to hear the results. Who's going to tell her?"

"I think I should," said Dr. Rheindollar. "I want you and Debra there as support. Wait for me in the family room in pediatrics."

We left the room and stood in the hall hugging each other for emotional as well as physical support, crying silently.

* * *

Dale said he had an appointment and would see her in the evening. Debra and I looked at each other as Debra sighed deeply, shaking her head as we walked across to the hospital from the conference room.

"How has she gotten so close to you, Debra?" I asked.

"At first, I was touched because she had no one else. After spending time with her, I saw how strong she was. She's a lot like me."

As we stood waiting for the elevator to pediatrics, I looked at the purple hippopotamus and green frog painted on the wall,

Disney versions of African animals. Today these bright animals were a sad reminder that Dayou would never see Africa again.

We finally arrived at the family room for those with seriously ill children. People, who had been waiting for a long time, sat with pillows and food, while others, exhausted, had their chairs pushed back and were sleeping. I drank it all in, realizing Debra and I were just beginning to get a taste of what it was like to have a terminally ill child.

Debra continued, "Carolyn, I've told Dayou at every crisis, 'Dayou, we're not giving up.' Now, I can't say that anymore. What's left to do?"

Suzanne hurried in the door and said, "Dr. Rheindollar wants you to come immediately."

Dr. Rheindollar stood at the foot of the bed looking helpless as he watched Dayou bending over, shaking with sobs. Her knees were drawn up and her hair braided and pulled to the back, her brown skin a sharp contrast with the white sheets. Debra and I put our arms around her and just held her. Finally, Dayou sat up and lowered her feet to the floor.

We murmured over and over, "We're so sorry. We love you."

Dr. Rheindollar walked to the door and stood there for several minutes looking back at the three of us. I wondered what he was thinking. Would he hear those sobs all night, see her shoulders shaking? The doctor raised his hand in farewell and closed the door.

Dayou looked up at Debra and cried, "Are we giving up yet?"

"No, Baby, we're not giving up." She tightened her arms around her. "We are not."

* * *

The previous May, when Dayou was hospitalized, word had spread through our church that she was seriously ill. One of the deacons, Bill Bumpus, Lois's husband, called the other deacons together in the early evening to pray for Dayou. I was with her at the hospital. Bill told me that some of them left the pews and knelt at the front of the church asking God for a miracle for this precious child.

They had prayed, but Dayou had gotten sicker, and, now, the worst news yet.

* * *

The next day I went back to the hospital. It seemed ironic that after months of trying to make contact with her family, a letter from her half-brother Peter arrived that day through the Red Cross. Debra brought it by. Dayou handed it to me as I came to her bed. I read silently.

> *From: Peter Ballah Kolo,*
> *Date of Birth: July 26, 1949*
> *Totota, Lower Bong County*
>
> *Dear Miss. Brenda Deese,*
> *We the family of Dayou (Layou) Tucker have received your letter dated May 20, 1997,*
> *seeking for information as to whether or not the parents are alive or living.*
> *You will please be informed all living and concern about her condition. We say*
> *many thanks to you for the concern you have for our daughter and sister. We are praying God that she will get well.*
> *Below are the family names:*
> *(1) Nylia Kolo – Father*
> *(2) Sangay Kolo – Mother*

(3) Miata Briggs – Aunt
(4) Peter B. Kolo – Elder Brother   July 10, 1997

Peter was her father's oldest son. Dayou described him as being in his fifties. Immediately, I noticed he listed the spelling of their dad's name as "Nylia Kolo" which was different from what Rev. Karnley had thought. Her mother's name was written as "Sangay Kolo," which we did have.

I handed Dayou the letter, and she moved it to the side to keep her tears from smearing the words as her fingers touched their names. She always said that if she had to die, she wanted to be at home with these people who had loved her first. She held the letter and reread it many times, the poignant ache for her missing family visible on her face.

Finally, looking up, she said, "I wish Peter had said more."

I knew she wanted so much more. Maybe Red Cross messages had to be short. Was it beyond coincidence that this had been written in July, but reached Dayou just when she needed the support of her family most? God's mercies were great.

"Will you answer the letter?" I asked.

"Mrs. Noell, can you go to the apartment and get some pictures for me? I want to send one of me as a cheerleader in the eighth grade and the picture of me in the long, blue dress made at the ROTC dance. After you get the pictures, we'll write the letter." Her voice choked and we remained silent for a while.

"I don't know why this is happening to me. I wonder if the reason I can't get a transplant is because I'm from Africa? When I'm alone I go over and over what Dr. Rheindollar told me," Dayou said.

"Exactly what reasons did he give you?" I asked.

"I'd been waiting for him to come in since you and Pastor Dale and Miss Debra had left the room. Dr. Rheindollar finally came through the door and held both my hands. He knows that

I'm from Africa, but he always says, 'You're not from here. Tell me where you came from.' I had really thought he'd come to tell me good news, but I was almost afraid to breathe."

"When he spoke, he said, 'Dayou, there are lots of people waiting for a liver, and never enough for the numbers of people who are desperately in need of a transplant. It would be hard for someone from another country to get one.' I held my breath even longer. Then he said, 'I think your hepatitis would return after surgery, which would leave you sicker than you are now.' He took a deep breath and held my hand tighter as he said, 'I cannot recommend a transplant for you.'"

"I knew what that meant," Dayou continued slowly. "Tears poured out as I thought, Dear God, why? This is not fair. I'm sixteen years old. I've tried so hard to get this far." Her voice broke.

Both of us were quiet. I turned toward the window to wipe away my own tears.

"Did Pastor Dale come last night?" I asked.

"Yes, after supper."

"What did he say?"

"That we have asked God for help, and He is in charge, regardless of how it seems to us."

* * *

Dayou had diarrhea and got tired of frequently getting up to go to the bathroom. She wanted to live and getting so weak scared her. She had to push herself to move, but move she did, slow step by slow step.

Days dragged along. Some nights Lois Bumpus and I stayed at the hospital. Sunday, Lois came late in the afternoon. She was planning to stay until eleven, and after supper suggested they watch "Touched by an Angel," but Dayou didn't want to see it.

Lois told me later that she had wondered if it was because of the death angel Michael.

One night I came in to find Dayou asleep and Lois on her way out, so I cuddled up in the recliner with a blanket. About two-thirty, Dayou got up to go to the bathroom and was confused about how to get there. I knew the liver failure was affecting her thinking processes.

I remembered that earlier the social worker had talked about sending Dayou to some kind of home for seriously ill children. I wondered if this would be ahead for Dayou or if she would be placed in a nursing home.

I thought back to when Dayou had told me about a surgeon named Dr. Poplawski, who had come by on his rounds. Dayou said she had asked him about getting a liver, and he had told her, "We don't give our livers to aliens."

That remark had hurt deeply. Aliens to her were creatures from outer space that have antennae and make weird beeping noises. She was a person with feelings. Anger ran over Dayou and me every time we thought about it.

Carol, Pastor Dale's wife, came into Dayou's room with a gift. It was a black doll with a pretty face and beautiful baby clothes. Dayou held it until supper. It was a girl, but it reminded her of her little brother at home in Africa and how she had loved playing with him.

* * *

Tom and I planned a short mountain trip, deciding to go while Dayou was still in the hospital. In my head, I was going over plans to bring her to our house. If Lois and Debra were willing to stay with us, two people could be on duty while the third slept. There were unanswered questions about the distance and whether Hospice would be less available in Davidson.

I was torn about leaving Dayou and could not have agreed to the trip if she hadn't had such a great support system with Debra, Pastor Dale, Lois and others. If we brought her to our house, I thought the days ahead would be hard physically and emotionally.

While we were away, Dayou was on my mind constantly. On the second day, we went to Grandfather Mountain, and I wondered if Dayou would like the swinging bridge, or if she'd be scared when it swayed. I felt the age of these mountains and thought of the sorrows they had taken in for hundreds of years.

Tom maneuvered the steep, curvy roads on the way down to the small zoo. I especially wanted Dayou to see the animals. There were bear cubs playing, attacking each other with boundless energy, energy that belonged to the young, energy that should have belonged to Dayou.

After the third night, Tom and I decided to go to home to face whatever needed to be done.

14

CHANGES

The Transplant Floor

They wait in hospital rooms,
not wishing for another's death,
but waiting for it,
so they can live.

Dayou woke up in the hospital feeling weaker than the day before. Debra sat in the recliner near the window.

Dr. Rheindollar walked into her room quietly. He stopped at the foot of her bed and said, "Dayou, I have some news, some good news."

She studied his face. He was smiling, but in a different way. It was almost as if he had a special secret. What now? Could she believe anything good was going to happen? She wondered if he'd say they were sending her to some kind of home, and he'd try to make her believe it would be good. She was afraid to hear, unable to keep her eyes off his as the sun coming through the blinds made lines across his face.

With caution, Dayou said, "What kind of good news?"

He moved closer to her, clearing his throat as he took her hand in both of his. Looking her in the eyes and squeezing her hand, he said, "Dayou, you are going to be put on the transplant list."

She couldn't believe her ears. She searched his face with her deep brown eyes, wondering if she had just heard correctly or if this were a cruel joke to get her hopes up.

Dr. Rheindollar couldn't believe her lack of reaction and asked, "Did you hear what I said? You're going to be put on the transplant list."

Debra started to grin and in seconds was yelling and hugging Dr. Rheindollar.

Dayou was too weak to yell, but she lay there smiling up at everyone.

Dr. Rheindollar explained to Debra, "I couldn't get her off my mind. I called the transplant center in Omaha and the Medical College of Virginia. The doctor I talked to in Omaha said he was coming to Charlotte the next day for a conference, and I met with him when he got to town. Both centers have tried a new procedure, and they think it will work. In fact, the Medical College of Virginia says that if there is not a surgeon in Charlotte who will try this, they will do it, if we bring her up there. But we do have a surgeon, and I'm working on the insurance."

Dayou's uncle came into the hall. Debra cried and hugged him. James Tucker thought Dayou had died. He raised his hand toward his mouth and stopped it in mid-air. A slow smile spread across his face as Debra's words sunk in.

* * *

The hospital staff moved Dayou to the floor with the people who were waiting for transplants. She was excited but almost afraid to get too happy, knowing that some people die waiting for an organ.

On that floor, the walls next to the hall were glass, and she could see very sick people in the rooms across from her. Nurses rushed in and out, and family members hovered over the beds with worry lines on their foreheads. Sometimes the curtains were closed quickly.

Debra, Pastor Dale, Lois, James Tucker and I visited Dayou, along with others. Since she didn't feel like talking, nobody stayed long. On Saturday, a lot of Liberians who live in Charlotte came, including Nancy and two other girls, Special and Mercy. The fact that they all stood around the bed and stared down at her bothered Dayou. Back home, families did this when someone was dying. They brought African food with them, but the nurses wouldn't let Dayou eat it because it was too spicy.

Dayou begged for fruit and was always thirsty. She felt depressed because she'd been sick so long. At night, she would lie in her room with the only light coming in from the hall. A young, black woman with a small frame and short hair came down the hall and stopped at her door. Her name was Tonya and she was the secretary for Dayou's floor. Dayou thought she was very pretty.

Tonya talked to Dayou and asked if she liked to watch movies. Dayou had said, "Yes, anything would be better than this." Tonya brought Dayou movies and talked to her every day. But the best thing they did was make a transplant bracelet out of some small, multicolored beads that Tonya brought in. Tonya said they would make matching bracelets, so when Dayou wore hers on the day of the transplant, she would be reminded that Tonya would also be wearing hers, and they would be connected in thought and spirit.

While they strung the beads, Tonya shared with Dayou that she was an English major at Winthrop University, going to school during the day and working at the hospital on the three to eleven shift. Dayou also learned that Tonya had a dog named Katy.

Dayou loved hearing about Tonya's life. She felt not much was happening in her own, that she was in waiting mode.

15

TURNAROUND

Surgery

Tonya beams.
"Remember, tomorrow
we wear transplant bracelets."
Her fingers touch my ankle as she fastens mine.

The answering machine flashed as I came into the kitchen with armloads of jackets and groceries. Tom and I had left the mountains about three o'clock.

The first call was from Debra saying, "Call me as soon as you get in." The second was Lois saying the same thing. There were two more from Debra. One said, "Everything has changed. Call me." There was one from Dale. "Has anybody called you about Dayou?" he asked.

My stomach tightened. I called Debra and left a message on her pager. Lois was not home. There was no answer at Dale's house. I tried Dayou's room at the hospital. Another patient answered. I didn't know what to think. But all the voices on the answering machine were cheerful.

The phone rang as soon as I put it down. Debra said, "Carolyn, you won't believe what's happened. Dayou has been put on the transplant list."

"Ahh," came out as I took a quick breath. "What on earth happened?" I felt light with this new hope.

She said, "I don't know, except that we are witnessing a miracle. The doctor came in this morning and said he had not been able to get Dayou off his mind, and he'd been on the phone to other transplant centers. Everything is a 'go.' He has a surgeon and the insurance company has agreed to the surgery. Dayou has already been moved to the transplant floor. Now, it's a waiting game to see if a liver will be available before it's too late."

I watched a ladybug slowly crawling up the door frame by the phone. It was a perfect copy of all its brothers and sisters. The tiny, round body stopped and waited.

"I can't believe this," I said. I felt giddy, as if my head were too light. "I'm so happy for her. How is she?"

"She's thrilled but still as sick as when you left. She knows she may not make it unless she gets a liver soon. The diarrhea is terrible and her stomach is swelling."

"I'll see her in the morning," I said.

"You can go in during certain times – like when she was in Intensive Care. It's not necessary for us to sit with her now because she has a nurse assigned to her. I'll be over there during my lunch hour," said Debra.

I hung up the phone noticing "Miss Lady" was almost to the top of the door. I wondered about her patient climbing when she had the ability to fly.

I ran upstairs to tell Tom. Unpacking, with hands full of socks and underwear, he stopped and held his position as I talked.

"That's wonderful," he said. "The best news I've heard in a long time. It's hard to believe everything changed while we were gone."

We crawled into bed thinking about a different plan. Where would Dayou go for recovery when the transplant was over? How near the hospital would she need to be?

For the next three weeks, I was in and out of Carolinas' Medical, coordinating trips to Charlotte with visiting times. Dayou wanted rice and chicken, which I cooked for her without salt. Rice was a staple for Liberians. She asked for a favorite dish, but then ate only a few bites. She also wanted fruit and popsicles. I wondered if she craved the acid in fruit. Her liquid intake was limited. Food rules were enforced more strictly since she was now on the transplant list.

On the last Sunday in October, I stopped by on my way to church. Dayou was smiling, out of bed, at least long enough to go to the bathroom, and she seemed stronger than usual. I kept thinking how good it would be for her to get a liver soon – soon being that day or Monday. I prayed constantly that it would happen, yet this wish was two-pronged because I knew somebody would have to die to make this possible. I wondered who would have to give up laughing and loving family in order for Dayou's life here to go on.

* * *

It was October 27th and Dayou had been on the transplant floor about three weeks. She knew she was the first one on the list at Carolinas' Medical and at University Memorial in Chapel Hill.

Tonya called Dayou after supper. "I have something to tell you," she said.

"What is it?" Dayou asked.

"Wait 'til I get there. I'll tell you then."

While she waited, the nurse began doing some things she had not done before. She was giving Dayou different medicines, one pill after the other. Dayou said, "What's going on? You already drew fluid from my stomach today. What's all this about?"

She paused, "You have a liver. Your surgery will be tomorrow."

These words ran through Dayou's body like an electric current. She was scared, but so happy. She was too weak to get out of bed, so she started clapping her hands and smiling as she proclaimed, "Thank you, God." This time Dayou didn't ask "Why?"

Tonya came rushing in. She looked at Dayou and knew she was too late to give her the news. She let her pocketbook slide to the floor and leaned over the bed to hug her. Neither of them could speak. They smiled at each other and wiped tears with the backs of their hands.

Tonya picked up the box of beads and lifted out the bracelets. "Let's put yours on your ankle," she said. Her fingers connected the strings. "Don't forget. We both wear these tomorrow."

* * *

Tuesday morning my phone rang. It was Debra, barely able to contain her excitement. "Carolyn, we have a liver. She will be taken into the operating room at one o'clock."

"We'll be there," I said. "I'll call Lois."

I ran upstairs, filled with happiness and fear, yelling for Tom to get ready.

16

THE LONG DAY

Afterwards

My church family
watches, nurses roll
me into Recovery,
IV's sway, wheels creak.
Everyone is choked,
silent with tears and prayers.

Tom and I picked Lois up outside Hoerst-Celanese where she works part-time. When we got to the surgical waiting room, Dayou had already been taken in. Pastor Dale, Paul Staggs, the youth director, Debra and Bobbi Williams, the mother of a teenager at church, were with her when she went to sleep.

We settled ourselves on one side of the waiting room, piling books and newspapers around us, guarding Coke cans. Seven of us sat together. Debby and Suzanne from the transplant team came to tell us the operation might take twelve to fifteen hours.

"We talked with the family of the donor last night," they explained. "We told them what this would mean to a sixteen-year-old girl. They agreed to it, but they wanted to remain anonymous."

95

Dale said he would like to write a letter on behalf of the church.

Debby smiled. "That's a good idea," she said. "We'll send it to the family."

The transplant team ladies talked about after-care and told us they would go over everything with us in detail later.

I felt a restless tension while we read, talked, ate snacks. I was sorry I didn't get here in time to see Dayou. About three o'clock, a young man from Liberia, who was a technician in the operating room, came out to report that her surgery had begun. He seemed especially interested in her case. All afternoon and evening he came by whenever he could to let us know how things were progressing.

We had not settled the question of where Dayou would go for recovery. Debra, Bobbi and I talked about our house, mine and Tom's, but decided it was too far from the hospital. Three mornings a week she would have to be at the lab by seven o'clock. Debra had an upstairs bedroom, but we didn't know if Dayou would be able to climb steps by release time.

Bobbi Williams said, "She can come to my house, but I'll be at work during the day." Bobbi's son, Drew, is fifteen and several of the teenagers from church live close enough to drop by. We felt Dayou needed some support from kids her age.

A plan was worked out. Debra would take care of hospital lab visits. Lois and I would alternate staying at Bobbi's house on the other days. I would continue tutoring her as soon as she felt well enough, and I would take the responsibility for getting a teacher for homebound students.

Sometime during the afternoon, Dr. Rheindollar came by. This was my first time to see him since the decision had been made to do the transplant. I hugged him in *thanks*.

Members of our group took turns going to the cafeteria for supper, so someone would always be in the waiting room. Other people from church began arriving. There were probably fifteen or more of us. People waiting for other patients had left, so we had the room to ourselves.

About nine o'clock, a nurse reported that all was going well and the surgeons were ready to close. The transplant had taken less time than they had anticipated. The prognosis was good and Dayou was doing fine. The room spontaneously burst into cheers and clapping.

At 10:15, Dr. Poplawski, the surgeon, came into the room. Everyone stood and moved closer to hear what he had to say. "Dayou is doing extremely well. We had a good liver. It's a miracle she's still here. When I touched her liver, it came apart in my hands. I don't know how she lived to get the transplant."

"Having said that, please know it doesn't mean we're out of the woods. The next few days will be critical. Remember, we always live with the possibility of rejection." We nodded. None of us wanted to think about that possibility.

"She will be rolled down this hall in a few minutes. If you like, you may line up outside to see her. You can not touch her or stop the staff who will be taking her to Recovery."

We shook hands with the surgeon, thanking him for being willing to give Dayou this new chance. I remembered what he had said about no livers for aliens and knew he had more than redeemed himself.

We walked out and stood side by side in the hall thinking we would cheer or applaud. As the bed came through the doors with IV bags swinging and we saw Dayou's face, nobody could speak.

The only sound was the clank of the bed, the swish of the respirator and the rubber soles of the attendant's shoes. We watched Dayou's dark features against the white sheets and knew we were seeing a miracle of God and of medicine.

After the doors to Intensive Care banged shut, we held our places. People were reaching for tissue or wiping eyes with the

97

backs of hands. When Dale was able to speak, he said, "Let's pray together." We moved out of the main hallway to the carpeted area outside the waiting room. Dale reached out to those on either side of him, and we formed a circle of clasped hands. He looked at each of us, and we returned tearful smiles, some moving heads from side to side in amazement. I looked down at the blue-green carpet, moved by what I saw as evidence of God's power. As we bowed our heads, we heard soft footsteps. The operating room technician from Liberia came around the corner. He separated two hands and stepped into the circle.

* * *

Tom and I took the elevator down. As the door opened we saw James Tucker waiting to get on. We stepped out beside him and I asked, "Are you just getting here?"

"No. I've been trying for hours to find out where everybody was waiting. I went home and called Martha. She didn't know where you were, so I came back to the waiting room on the fifth floor. But no one could tell me anything."

"Oh, James, I'm so sorry. We were on that floor but in a separate room. Dayou is out of surgery – just came out. She's doing well. The surgeon spoke to us. He said the next few days will be critical, but everything looked as good as possible right now."

Tom reached up and put his arm around James's shoulder as he said, "James, let us go back up to Recovery with you, and maybe you can go in to see Dayou for a minute."

"Thank you. I would appreciate that."

On the way up, I told James the plans for after-care and apologized for not having had a way for him to find us. We located a nurse and left James talking to her in the hall.

17

OUT OF THE HOSPITAL

Rx. for the Medicine Man's Daughter

Prograf (100 mg.)
CellCept (500 mg.)
Lasix (40 mg.)
Prednisone (15 mg.)
Augmintin (500 mg.)
K-Dur (20 mg.)
Mycelex Troche

I got a cell phone Friday so I could call Bobbi if I were tied up in traffic between Davidson and Mint Hill, a suburb of Charlotte. I would be able to give her my location, so when I was close, she could go on to work. I had a key to the house.

After the first few days Dayou would be well enough to be left alone for a short time, and Bobbi and Randy could leave at their regular times.

I called Bobbi Monday morning when I was near her neighborhood. Fifteen minutes later I drove into the yard in the coolness of November and noticed the stack of firewood outside the back door. I pushed past the cats that were leg weaving, hoping to squeeze into the house. Unlocking the door, I went in through the office where the computer screen glowed in the

99

darkened room. There was one step up to the dining area, and beyond that, images flickered on the TV in the den. Dayou was lying on the couch. I called her name as I walked in.

"Hey," she responded.

"How are you feeling?"

"I don't know. Not too good I guess."

Behind the glass doors, logs were burning in the fireplace. I moved closer wanting the comfort of fire.

Victoria, the Williams' English pug, scrambled out of an easy chair and wiggled all her blond self to greet me. She snorted when she breathed.

"Are you warm enough?"

"Yeah, I keep this blanket over me."

"Have you had any breakfast?"

"No, I start my medicines at eight o'clock. Then I wait a while, and with breakfast there is another set of pills. Check my chart on the cabinet."

I saw it taped above a dozen dark bottles with white tops and labels. Some were larger than any prescription bottles I'd seen. I studied the chart and put the first set to be given to one side.

"It's almost eight, Dayou. I'll get you a glass of water." I washed my hands at the kitchen sink and dried them on a paper towel. Then I opened the bottle of Prograf (100 mg.) and shook out a pill. The Prograf and 500 mg. of CellCept were to prevent rejection. The last was Lasix to keep her from retaining fluid.

Dayou took half of a 40 mg. tablet. She swallowed the medicine and lay back on the pillow.

I sat down and rubbed Victoria. She had a kennel between the dining area and the den, but slept on the loveseat snoring loudly. She woke up and decided to get on the couch with Dayou.

"Get off," Dayou yelled, pushing her back. "Get away from me."

"She likes you, Dayou. She just wants to be friendly."

"I don't like dogs. I don't want her over here. She needs to stay on her couch."

I heated water in the microwave for hot chocolate and opened the refrigerator to scout possibilities for lunch. There was a good-looking dish of macaroni and cheese, but I knew Dayou hated cheese. There was a plastic bowl with stew beef and gravy. I spotted some orange Jell-o and assorted vegetables. Dayou was a picky eater. I didn't know if she'd touch any of this.

I sat at the table with my mug and read the paper as I sipped my drink with tiny bits of powder – wet but not completely dissolved – floating on top.

I saw a picture of a lady in a coat and scarf kneeling and digging in rubble. The caption explained that a plane crashed into her apartment building in Russia, and she was searching for some sign of her thirteen-year-old son. I could only see the profile of her face. I tried to imagine her horror.

Soon after I retired from teaching, I began writing poetry and nonfiction. The images from the account of the plane crash turned in my mind with the possibility of a poem.

At nine, Dayou agreed to some orange juice and cereal, so she could take the Prednisone (15 mg.) to prevent rejection, Augmintin (500 mg.) to prevent infection, Bactrim, a sulfa, to keep down bacterial infection, and K-Dur (20 mg.) which was potassium. Afterwards, she sucked on a Mycelex Troche, which was to keep her from getting a yeast infection while taking the antibiotics.

Suzanne from the transplant center called to check on Dayou, to be certain she was taking the medicine properly. Suzanne's number was posted by the phone so I could find it immediately if anything went wrong. She reminded me that Dayou must be at the lab at Carolinas Medical by seven o'clock Tuesday morning. I assured her that Debra would be bringing her and that all of her days were covered between Lois, Debra and me, with Bobbi home on the weekends. Other people from our church were on call if we needed relief.

After I hung up, I wondered if the transplant team was still concerned about us doing what we had promised. Perhaps they thought we were do-gooders who would soon tire of the project. I understood their doubts, because things have been dropped by well-intentioned folks.

Everyone made sacrifices to care for Dayou. Debra arranged to have her messages taken and made no appointments on lab days. She had to leave home by six o'clock in the morning or earlier to make the seven o'clock lab time. Lois, who worked part-time, would juggle her schedule so she could be here on her duty days. Bobbi worked for a company that transports and develops film for Eckerd Drug Stores. She went in to work early and usually got off by mid-afternoon. Her family was making major adjustments to commit to caring for Dayou.

Everything was on hold in my life until we got Dayou well and back in school. I had stopped doing tours for third graders at Latta, an 1800's plantation house, and, for these weeks, I gave up my book club and writer's group.

At twelve-thirty we reviewed the possibilities for lunch. Dayou decided on a baked potato which I cooked in the microwave. After she finished about half of that, she agreed to eat a peeled and cut-up orange. She then had the multivitamin, Augmentin again and Mycelex Troche.

Dayou slept some after lunch with the TV volume turned down. While she was asleep, I got on the computer and worked on a poem about the woman searching for her son. I thought about her digging in the cold, searching for a cap, a familiar sweater, his soccer ball. Between phone calls, I kept writing about her.

When Dayou woke, about two, I asked her about taking a shower, which she agreed to do. She walked slowly and slightly bent over to the shower off Bobbi's bedroom. I turned on the water and adjusted it to the right temperature.

Dayou took off her gown and stepped into the shower. In a short while she was ready to come out. She was shaking, bending over protecting a purple, jagged scar across her stomach.

"Are you cold?" I asked.

"Cold and weak," she said.

She put on her gown and by the time she got back to the couch, she said she was exhausted.

About mid-afternoon, Drew came in from Independence High and dumped a load of books on the table before going into the den to ask Dayou how she was. He got a snack and took the dog out. Drew is in ninth grade.

A few minutes later, Bobbi got home. We talked about Dayou's food and medications. Bobbi said, "Saturday night, Dayou woke me and said she was having chest pain. She had been crying and thought she was having a heart attack. She had asked about going to the emergency room, but I suggested we try one thing first. I gave her some Mylanta, thinking it could be indigestion, and I told her if she wasn't better in a few minutes I would get some help. Sure enough, in about twenty minutes, she was okay or as okay as she could be this soon after surgery. Dayou didn't want to go back to her room to sleep. She said she was more comfortable on the couch so she stays in the den every night. "I don't mind," Bobbi said.

Dayou's friends were home from school now, so some of them began calling. She was not very talkative, so the conversations were short.

I got my things together and headed out. Drew was doing homework at the table; Bobbi and Dayou were watching General Hospital and talking about the characters. I told them I'd be back on Wednesday, pushed the cats back with my foot and closed the storm door.

As I drove back to Davidson, I felt relief that the first day had gone well and that Dayou seemed to be stronger than I expected. I was encouraged that she could take a shower.

I knew she had a long way to go. But Bobbi was taking good care of her, and things seemed peaceful and settled at her house.

18

RECOVERY
MOVES FORWARD

At Bobbi's House

"I move slowly,
do English grammar,
heal day by day,
eat lunch at the Chinese buffet
on Eastway Drive."

Dayou still rested on the couch much of the time, but for longer and longer periods she could sit at the dining room table and work on English. A teacher for the homebound came twice a week and left assignments. He was unable to stay long enough to give her much help, but he did ask questions about her grammar lessons so he could assess progress. He was in contact with her teachers at West Charlotte. Dayou was given credit for JROTC this semester and, if she completed the written work, for one semester of tenth grade English and for remedial reading. This would allow her to graduate on time if she went to one session of summer school after tenth grade.

On the days I stayed with Dayou, we worked for an hour in the morning and at least an hour after lunch. I tried to be sensitive about how hard I could push her at each stage to find a balance between fatigue and wasting time. Each day when I left, I made suggestions about what she could work on before I came back. Sometimes Randy, Bobbi's husband, helped after he came home from work. He was good with words. He worked crossword puzzles in ink because he never had to erase.

On a Wednesday in early December, I came in at three o'clock to relieve Lois. Bobbi planned to go from work to church that day. She is the church treasurer and usually writes checks before supper. There were boxes of Christmas cards on the dining room table with stacks of envelopes addressed and stamped. I recognized Dayou's large, rounded letters on some.

Lois said, "I worked on my cards today, and Dayou has done hers, also. I brought some extras. Dayou read the messages and selected the best ones for her doctors, nurses, social workers and friends."

Lois always thought of the things that I didn't, like making certain Dayou expressed appreciation to folks, ironing her clothes and hemming skirts or pants. I zeroed in on English and math homework. I thought how kids really do need a village.

Within a few days we began to take some trips. Dayou was up more, taking the dog out and keeping wood on the fire. She also helped Bobbi with laundry on the weekends.

On Monday afternoon, we went to the library at Mint Hill. I wanted Dayou to choose some books for pleasure reading to cut down on TV watching. We stopped by the grocery store and she picked several frozen entrees, which could be used for lunch. We also got junk food. Her favorite was pork rinds.

Dayou went to the hospital every other day, and afterwards Debra took her places, but this was my first time to have her in the car and it was good to see her out.

The following week we drove to her favorite Chinese restaurant for lunch and then to Eastland Mall for shopping. We were looking for clothes that were stylish, but loose enough not to irritate her incision. We kept searching for denim overalls that would fit that description. She wanted to settle for some that were too tight, by my standards, but I talked her into waiting and trying again later. I thought the scarred area might be sensitive for several months and that when she went back to school, she needed clothes she could wear all day without a problem.

I was surprised by her stamina, and as we shopped I asked if she felt up to walking to another store. She said, "Yes."

Back at Bobbi's there was a call from Christy and Jay Godwin asking what Dayou wanted for Christmas. Year before last, Christy came with a church group to tutor at our church and grew close to Dayou. Her fiancé Jay become part of the relationship. Christy grew up in Nigeria, the daughter of missionaries, so she feels a kinship with Dayou. Throughout the illness and rehab period, they had kept in touch.

The first Saturday Dayou was out of the hospital, Christy brought a cake she had made. She was a newlywed, and I doubted she had done a lot of baking, so I thought it was special that she made this effort. Dayou's bedroom furniture, which had been moved from the apartment to Bobbi's house, had been bought by Christy and Jay.

A few days later, Bobbi and I talked about when Dayou would go home. Bobbi said she wanted Dayou to stay as long as she needed help, but felt it was important that she get back into her routine at home and become independent as soon as possible.

I knew that Dayou did not want to think about going back. She loved the "mothering" at Bobbi's and the feeling of being in a family. She said the apartment had bad memories for her because she had been so sick there. I believed she was afraid to be alone. Her uncle worked two jobs and had a lady friend. At the same time, I thought Bobbi should be the one to call the shots, and I knew the arrangement there was temporary.

As Dayou got stronger, she and Drew picked at each other as brothers and sisters do. I wondered if this bothered Bobbi when she came in tired. On the other hand, I knew Bobbi had good people skills and was quite effective communicating with teenagers. She could always stop anything that got to be too much.

The decision was made to move Dayou back to the apartment before Christmas and Bobbi would invite her to spend Christmas Eve and Christmas Day with her family. Dayou was agreeable, although she was unsure about coming back for the holidays.

She said, "Mrs. Noell, I know everyone in this country makes a big deal over Christmas morning. I see stories and commercials on TV where the children get up and run to the tree squealing. In my country, we didn't do that. I don't even feel comfortable with it. I know all of you want this to be exciting for me, but what I expect at Christmas is different from what you expect and are used to. Christmas and Thanksgiving are just not to me what they are to you."

"How would Christmas be at home?" I asked.

"Well, when I was a child, I would say to a relative or close friend, 'My Christmas is on you.' If the adult said, 'Okay,' that meant they would buy a gift for me. It would not be wrapped in fancy paper. Maybe just handed to me in a bag."

"What about food?"

"We would have a big meal on the afternoon of Christmas Day. Before that, children went from house to house and were given treats. My friend and I used to sing for the neighbors as they passed out sweets."

"So you see, everything is so different here that it makes me sad. I think I would feel better to be alone and not have to pretend it's fun."

Debra suggested that Dayou have some of her friends from Liberia at the apartment on Christmas Eve and that they open their gifts to each other, have some party foods and that she go to Bobbi's the next day. This was the compromise.

I gave Dayou a green warm-up suit, a necklace and a photo album. On the last two pages I put two poems I had written. One was about the war in Liberia, and the other one I wrote on the night of her surgery.

I often teased her about being a captive audience. I used to read a poem to her after we finished her homework or once when she was sitting on the examining table in the emergency room waiting for the doctor. Then I said, "Dayou, you can't escape now. I'm going to read a poem to you."

She had been polite about my work before. She liked these poems. They were about her, the concern people had for her and the country she loved.

Uncivil War

Rebel gunfire shatters the afternoon.
A woman cooking, hides, rice scatters,
children playing war, run,
men go deeper into the bush.
Soldiers storm the village, grab food from pots,
steal chickens, toss out bedding.
The woman's husband is led away
for tomorrow's execution.
Liberia is watered with tears.

Helicopter blades churn leaves and dust.
Relief workers, missionaries are lifted out
with powerful airborne motors.
Survivors huddle in refugee camps,
skirting the edges of Monrovia,
baby chicks around a hen.

The woman hears a radio filled
with lost person pleas.
Handles of water buckets cut into her hands,
rice pings against the bottom of the cooking pot.

Hope Rushes In

As long as I know who I am
I'll remember tonight…
Dayou, sixteen, out of surgery,
IV bags swinging like udders.

A family gave their child's liver.
God and the transplant team
brought another chance.
Now we dream for her
about tenth grade,
her first job, falling in love.

She traveled out of war
in Liberia to Charlotte,
disease, relentless.
We, her church family, wait,
stand in the hall,
ready to clap, cheer.
Green coated O.R. workers
roll the creaking bed past.
Hushed by the miracle,
we study her sleeping face,
dark skin beautiful against white sheets.

19

ANGELS ALL AROUND

Jackson Calls

My sister Momi gone –
we played house,
fed our dolls mud pies.

Grandmother, gone, too,
with her country smell of
sundried flowers.

I'm empty now.

Sunday, Dayou's half-brother Jackson called from Liberia in the middle of the night. They talked for a while. She asked about the family. "How is Grandmother Briggs and my sister?" He didn't want to talk about them. She knew something was wrong.

"Tell me what's happened. I've got to know."

"Your Grandmother died."

"Oh, no."

"She died during the war, three years ago."

Sadness came over Dayou. She knew there would never be anyone to take up for her the way Grandmother Briggs did. She wanted so much to see her again. "What else?" she asked. "You haven't told me everything."

"It's Momi."

Dayou hesitated, then in a soft voice she said, "What?"

"She's gone, too."

Dayou sobbed, "My sister's gone? No, I can't believe it. She's only fourteen." Dayou was silent for a few seconds, trying to get her voice back. "Was it sickle cell?"

"I don't know – probably."

"If I had been able to get her over here, maybe the doctors could have helped her. I'm sure there are kids here who die from sickle cell, but I've never heard of anyone who did. I feel guilty that I got medical care and she didn't."

"Thank you, Jackson, for calling. I'll talk to you soon," Dayou said.

She sank down on the couch. "Grandmother Briggs, Momi, I feel so empty without you. I love you both so much," she sobbed. "It's hard to grieve over here by myself. I feel shaky, like I'm coming apart. I've got to find a way to go home. I've been away too long."

Momi always lived with her mom and grandmother on the farm. When Dayou came home from her aunt's house to visit, they got along fine for a few days. They pretended to cook and take care of doll children. After a while, they began to fuss and fight. Dayou wished she hadn't been mean to Momi.

She did a project on sickle cell for biology and kept hoping there would be a medicine she could send. Now it was too late. Death was so final. It ended chances to do things for people. It ended dreams.

Dayou was the only one living of the children her parents had together. There were dozens of half-brothers and sisters her dad had by other wives, but she felt cut off, like an orphan, with her last full-sister buried.

112

Jackson said her mother had two more children. This worried Dayou. Her mother should have stopped having children. She was healthy but her children were sick – born sick. Of course, the father of these babies was not Dayou's father.

* * *

Dayou's nose was bleeding when she was born. There were always times when it bled. Once, she remembered it didn't stop for a whole month. Dayou couldn't eat and lost so much weight her clothes didn't fit. Her dad made one of his wives cook some special food for her, but when Dayou put it in her mouth, she threw up.

They put charcoal up her nose to try to stop the bleeding. Other medicines were used, too, but sometimes it was so bad nothing would help.

There was talk that a curse had been put on the family and some said a life must be taken to remove it. Her mom's family didn't believe in witchcraft since they went to the Baptist Church.

What a shock for her mom to lose her mother and Momi. Grandmother Briggs was a strong-willed little lady. Dayou remembered one day her mother had been going to the river to wash clothes on the rocks.

Grandmother Briggs said, "Now you scrub my things good and use this soap, but first soak the stains on my apron, and make sure you get all the suds out with a good rinse." Mom had gone off and left the clothes in a pile on the floor. They had had their mother-daughter times.

Dayou used to carry a bucket of water so her grandmother could take a bath. The bathhouse floor was made of rock, and after her grandmother had soaped up, rainbow bubbles stood on the wet stone. Dayou had washed her grandmother's back, then used a dipper for rinsing. Afterwards, she loved to sniff the sachet bags her grandmother made from dried flowers, and kept with her clothes. They had a good country perfume.

When her grandmother had been a young woman she had found a snake in her bed one night. Her husband killed it, but she had always thought the spirit of the snake was in her body. Her fingers curled when she was old, and she had said, "Look, Layee. That's the snake in my body turning my fingers." Dayou thought it was arthritis, but her grandmother always believed it was the snake.

Her grandmother had hit her breasts and cried when she talked about her daughter who had left Liberia when she graduated from high school. She had gone to live in the U.S., but had not been to visit or written in years. Grandmother had wanted so much to hear from her.

Dayou picked up her English book from the coffee table and ran her fingers around the edge. Momi had been brought up very much the way her grandmother and mom had been. She had gone to school very little, probably because of her illness. Dayou thought about the differences in their lives, all she'd seen and had that Momi didn't know about.

She thought about going back for a visit, planning carefully how it would be. She'd go to Monrovia and rent a hotel room and the next day, get a car and driver to take her to Totota. She'd be careful what she ate and would make sure to take plenty of bottled water.

She wanted to dress nicely and look pretty when she went back. She'd get her hair braided and buy something pink. First, she'd go to Aunt Meatta's house in Totota. She knew her aunt would be so happy to see her. They'd hug and look at each other. She'd been the one who had raised Dayou.

Her house would smell good with special food she'd been cooking. Dayou knew she'd have rice with chicken and spinach, fruits and sweets.

114

They had not been on good terms when they had parted. When Dayou had returned hungry from Monrovia, her aunt had heard she had barely escaped death at the hands of the rebels, and she had wanted Dayou to stay with her. Aunt Meatta had worked for Tubman Farms. Dayou thinks she cooked for them. All she really knew was that her aunt always brought food home. She used to spoil Dayou and give her the best she could. It had upset her aunt when Dayou had left the village to go stay with her mom and grandmother.

Once, when her aunt came to the farm to visit, she wouldn't talk to Dayou or eat the food Dayou cooked for her. She was worried because Dayou had eaten something she was allergic to and had broken out in a rash. Meatta loved her and wanted to take care of her at her own house.

When Dayou was little, Aunt Meatta would come home from work and ask if her cousins had been mean to her. Dayou had always answered "Yes," even though it wasn't true. Then Dayou would be given special foods. Her aunt would buy her fry fish, bread or anything she wanted. She'd eat a little and then start playing with it on her plate. The cousins would say, "Can we have some?" Dayou would say, "No." Dayou thought of herself as a spoiled brat, but she knew her aunt would have a big smile when she saw her.

Her dad also had a house there so she might see him. If he were not in Totota, she'd find him in one of the villages. She imagined he'd grab her in a big hug and squeeze her tight. She knew he'd be happy, because she and her dad were close. She used to wonder if he would choose her to pass down the secrets of his medicine. But after thinking more about it, she believed it would be her half-brother Peter, who was the oldest and also very close to his father.

Her mom was still on her parents' farm. Dayou used to walk there in about forty-five minutes. It would only take a short time

115

by car. It would be wonderful. They'd talk and talk about everything. She had spoken to her mother once on the phone, but her accent had been heavy and she talked so fast, Dayou had to ask her to put her brother back on. She spoke Kpelle and her English was not as clear as Dayou was used to hearing.

Her little half-brother was nine now. He wouldn't remember her. Then, of course, she'd meet the two born since she left. The baby girl was two.

She ached to think how she'd miss seeing Momi. Dayou wanted to have cement put on her grave with angels all around. She'd arrange artificial flowers in vases and then sit down to talk to Momi, tell her how sorry she was for all the times she had fussed with her or had been mean to her. She'd ask Momi to forgive her. She planned to sit at the grave and talk for a long time.

She'd see everybody – how they had changed. In the evening, she'd have the driver take her back to Monrovia and the next day, she'd fly back to Charlotte.

She would feel strange being back there with the people and in the places she remembered. She was very different from the eleven-year-old who had left home. So much had happened to change her.

When she first came here, people had a lot of trouble understanding her. She spoke English but with an accent. Now she spoke much clearer. Then, this whole country had been a mystery to her. The food was different, she didn't know how the schools were set up, and she had been scared of being killed in the streets. Now it wouldn't be long before she would apply for citizenship.

She had been frustrated when she started school and couldn't read well or write correctly, but, now, she was in high school, and getting along okay. She had friends here. Her church family was important to her. She almost died from hepatitis, and she felt so much better since the liver transplant – better than she ever did growing up when she had been sick much of the time.

Everybody back in Liberia would be different, too. They were older, had been through the war and still suffered the aftermath. The pain of war went on and on.

Dayou wished she could get pictures of her family. Her aunt had said she would send some by express mail, so Dayou had sent her forty dollars to cover the mailing costs. Then her aunt had called and said she had given them to a girl, who was coming to the U.S. That girl had been on the plane from Ivory Coast that had gone down in the Atlantic last month. At night, Dayou thought of their precious faces deep in salt water.

20

FRIEND FROM HOME

Dr. Ardaiolo at Winthrop U.

He shows me the photos,
schools without roofs,
books locked up
by Taylor's government,
clinics with no equipment.
I turn my eyes away.

Dayou's shoes clattered down the metal steps from her apartment. She wore jeans and had her hair done up in back with two long strands on either side of her face. She carried a notebook and a black pocketbook with shoulder straps.

Tom and I greeted her as she crawled into the back seat, pushing aside the video camera.

"I don't have to be on camera, do I?" she asked.

"Of course you do," I replied. "You ask the questions, and Dr. Ardaiolo will answer. Tom will record the interview."

"Let me ask the questions from the side. He can be in the picture alone."

"No, you need to be seen. This is your graduation project."

As Tom pulled into afternoon traffic and headed for Interstate 77, I recalled the phone conversation with Dr. Ardaiolo, an administrator at Winthrop University. He had readily agreed to an interview when I told him a teenager from Liberia wanted to know about the status of schools in her country.

He said, "I would love to talk to her. That was my home when I was a teenager. My father managed Roberts Air Field for Pan-Am. A good number of whites did business in the country then. I went to school there in the eighth grade, came to the U.S. for high school and college but returned for summers and holidays until I was twenty-one. I consider myself a Liberian."

He had been curious about how I had located him.

"I spotted an article about your trip in the *New York Times*," I said. "It was picked up from the Rock Hill paper."

We had arranged a day and time to meet.

Dayou spoke from behind me, "Did you say Dr. Ardaiolo has pictures for me?"

"That's what he said," I assured her. "He was in Liberia a year ago this month. He went to Totota and the area near your village."

"Oh, my gosh."

"Have you seen any photographs of home since you left?"

"No, I have talked to some people who came to Charlotte after I did, but I haven't seen pictures. I only remember what it looked like in 1992."

"Do you want crackers or something to drink? I don't know how long this will take. Supper may be late."

"No thanks. I'm too nervous."

We merged onto I-77, and traffic slowed immediately. Tom and I checked the clock on the dash. We had less than thirty minutes to get to Rock Hill, find Winthrop University and Dr. Ardaiolo's office. He was a busy vice-president, and I didn't want to be late.

Dayou was quiet in the backseat reviewing her questions. We found the exit number and following internet directions pulled onto the campus. Dayou watched the buildings and students with great interest. I realized this was her first visit to a college campus. As we parked behind the student center, she asked if this was where the students lived.

Tom answered, "No, we are barely on time, so we can't look for dorms now." He carried the camera as we entered a side door.

Small groups of students were talking or watching TV. Dayou turned to look at each one. I knew she was checking out clothes and hair.

Dr. Ardaiolo's secretary greeted us. Within five minutes, he entered the room and reached out to shake hands with Dayou. As their hands separated, he informed her she had not given him a Liberian handshake.

She frowned, then quickly smiled and told him she had forgotten how it went.

He extended his hand again, snapping his fingers as he pulled away. Dayou tried a couple of times before she was successful.

"This fall I gave that handshake to a student from Liberia and she cried, saying it had brought back so many memories," he said, smiling at Dayou.

He invited us into his office. There was a desk at the entrance, a striped animal skin on the wall and African figures and bowls placed strategically around the room. In the adjoining room, a sofa sat in front of a large window, with two chairs grouped across from it.

He and Dayou took the chairs facing the last rays of December sun. Dr. Ardaiolo told Dayou he had pictures to show her after the interview. She smiled looking around the office.

Dr. Ardaiolo's manner with Dayou was gentle. He listened carefully to what she had to say.

She went over the questions with him and asked him to space his answers so the video would be about fifteen minutes long. She explained it would be presented with her paper.

121

He said his traveling companions had been a man from the university and a lady who had served in Liberia as a Peace Corps volunteer. They were members of a group called Friends of Liberia which raises money to restore schools and clinics.

He began, "In Monrovia, I found my old house. Jungle was overgrowing it. I knocked on the door to find a Nigerian peace keeper living there. I asked if I could look around. I said, 'You must let me. It was my house before it was yours.' He smiled and invited me in."

"Monrovia was so changed. The swimming pool where I spent wonderful hours was dry, and tall plants with big leaves pushed up where we had had tables and hammocks."

"Our group headed south along the coast to Buchanan. Armed guards stopped us often, demanding bribes. They said, 'Who are you?'"

"I said, 'I am a Liberian.'"

"The guards were skeptical, saying sternly, 'You don't look like one.'"

"Then I told them about Roberts Field and that I was a Friend of Liberia traveling to see the needs of the country, including the conditions of schools. Each one agreed to let us pass. They look to the U.S. to get them back on their feet, but this country has no plans to help."

I thought it was a miracle that an Italian-American could pass himself off as an African and travel safely. Dr. Adaiolo was so verbal, his answers so smooth, he gave the appearance of a rehearsed performance.

"Some of the schools we visited were without roofs. The children did not have books. They learned by rote from the teacher. Books from UNICEF were stacked in warehouses. The president, Charles Taylor, requires a payment of fifteen dollars for each book before they can be distributed. There were few jobs, little money."

122

I watched Dayou. She frowned with worry lines on her forehead.

"How about the teachers?" she asked.

"The teachers still work, although they have not been paid in a long time. The men wear ties and the women dresses. They seem to find some comfort in formality."

"We saw few whites. There were still some missionaries. They have the best schools, especially the Catholics."

"Liberia is now probably like South Carolina was following the Civil War, after Sherman marched through. I wonder if it will take one hundred and thirty years to recover."

Dayou shifted in her chair as she asked her last question, "When the U.S. sends aid to the Albanians and many other places, why don't they help Liberians? Two hundred and fifty thousand have been killed."

"Because we gave the last president, Samuel Doe, a half billion dollars, and it was embezzled, wasted. When Charles Taylor finished his education here and was positioning himself to fight for control, he received help from Gaddafi, who is no friend of ours."

"Another fact is that Liberia has nothing we need. Their rubber plantations are no longer important. We use synthetic rubber."

"Dayou, what I'm going to say, you'll find hard to hear. Whites still feel prejudice towards blacks."

Dayou nodded and looked down. "I know. African Americans here are even prejudiced towards Africans. A boy at school once said, 'You are no more than a dog.' He was as dark skinned as I am."

The interview ended on this note. Dr. Ardaiolo pulled out folding story boards with labeled pictures from different areas. Dayou bent over each one as he talked, seeing ravaged buildings, overgrown streets, burned houses. She spotted the clinic where she had been treated. A nurse was sterilizing equipment in an open tub. School walls were bare, without posters or chalkboards. There were no pictures of her mother's house but similar ones with zinc roofs and stucco walls. She saw the Coo-Coo's Nest near Totota. This was the former home of President Tubman. Now it belongs to Charles Taylor.

There were no photographs of her father's villages.

As Dr. Ardaiolo pointed out the destruction, Dayou said several times, "Oh, no." When he handed her individual pictures, she held them carefully, as if they were breakable.

Her dream had been to go home next summer after graduation. She wanted so much to see her parents. One of her sisters died and a brother was born last year. She wondered if she could communicate with her mother who speaks Kpelle. What would they think of her – the daughter who had escaped the war, had a liver transplant and would soon have a high school diploma? Would her step-brothers and sisters hate her for her privileges? She knew the visit would be short because she still needed regular medical care.

We said our "thank-yous" and "goodbyes" and went out to the car, shivering in dropping temperatures. Dayou sighed deeply as she settled into the back seat.

"What are you thinking?" I asked.

"I can't go home. I'm not ready to see my country like that. It hurts too much. I won't be going back after graduation."

21

THREATS AT SCHOOL

Scared

A girl threatens me.
I wish I could quit school
but graduation's in sight and
I won't give up the dream.

Dayou called at eleven-thirty in the morning. "I passed the English Competency Test." She sounded bubbly with excitement.

"That's great," I said, waiting for the next part.

"I missed math by only one point. I know I'll get it next time. It was number seven. I know exactly how I messed up on it."

"You're on the way. I know you'll make it. When do you take the math part again?"

"May 5th. Well, I better get back to class. I just wanted to tell you," Dayou said.

"I've been thinking about you this morning and wondering if you had heard. Thanks for calling. Did you hear anything from Harris Teeter?"

"No, I'm disgusted with them. I stayed at home my whole Easter break waiting for them to let me know about the drug test and if I had the job. I called back and the manager didn't even return my call. I'm not messing with them again. I called Wal-

Mart, and they said the assistant manager was doing orientation so I don't know. I'm still trying."

"Okay, I'll see you tomorrow afternoon."

"Okay, bye."

I thought about the excitement in Dayou's voice when she told me about the test. She clung to good news and moved on around the disappointments. Surely she'd graduate if she was this close. I couldn't stand to think about how hard it would be if she didn't.

On Wednesday, she and Tom and I went to the Diamond Restaurant for supper. It's a little neighborhood place on Commonwealth Avenue a few blocks from the church. They cook great vegetables, cornbread and biscuits, but you don't want to look around with a critical eye. There is a black-framed Grade A behind the counter, but everything is worn. Some of the booths seem to have been reupholstered but in the same drab green of the early fifties. The tile on the floor is worn down through several layers. Beside the front door is a yellow plastic dishpan filled with ice. This, along with brown plastic water pitchers, sits on shelves held together with silver duct tape.

It's definitely a seat-yourself place. We slipped into a booth by the door. Dayou looked around and said, "When was this place built?"

"About 1949," Tom said. "Probably the same time your apartment was. They just haven't been into too much renovation."

"It reminds me of places in Africa that get old and worn, and they just keep using them anyway."

Many of the customers had white hair and talked quietly or not at all. Several men straddled the round stools with chrome bands. They leaned over plates or cups of coffee.

A few women sat alone, one reading a paperback. A black family, with their young children, crowded the booth behind Tom. The waitresses called customers by name, chatted and asked about someone missing. I felt as if we were intruders at a family meal.

We studied the menu. Dayou asked about pickled beets and great northern beans. Tom explained what they were. She ordered hamburger steak, okra and, with my urging, green beans.

She picked up the vinegar jug. "What's that?" She giggled, holding it to the light.

There was a tiny something, no bigger than a bit of dust in the bottom. She shook it up and the speck drifted back to the bottom.

"Oh, no," Tom said. "Now Dayou won't eat here."

She smiled.

I told her how proud I was of her for staying in school. I said, "I know there have been times when you have wanted to quit."

"Yes, I want to right now." Dayou was turning the saltshaker in her hands.

"What's going on?"

"A girl in my class is threatening me. Last week, she was kicking her foot, and it was bumping my desk. I asked her to stop because I was trying to write. I wouldn't have minded if I hadn't been writing. She refused, so I moved my desk up and out of the reach of her foot. That made her mad for some reason. I didn't say anything to her. The next day the teacher asked me to pass out some papers. She wouldn't take hers."

"I laid it on the desk in front of her and it slipped off. When she picked it up, she shoved the desk into my back. I was sitting with one desk between us. It really hurt and the teacher saw what she did. She called her down and wrote a discipline referral. I went up to the office to Ms. Drakeford. You remember I've told you about her."

Dayou tried to line up grains of salt on the green tabletop. She moved her fingers back and forth straightening the line.

"I knew her at Piedmont when I was in middle school. She always helps me out if I have trouble. Well, I went to her office.

She's a secretary. I told her what happened, and she wrote a police report in case the injury turned out to be something that needed treatment."

"She gave the paper to the resource officer, and he called the girl out of class and talked to her. None of this was my idea, because I know that girl, and she will get a bunch of her friends and try to beat me up."

"The next day in class she was saying a bunch of stuff to me about how I had gotten her into trouble and that now she has a police record at school. Her friends were backing her up. I didn't say a word to them. They are not going to keep me from graduating this close to the end. Somebody threw a piece of gum and hit me on the head."

"One of my friends who rides on their bus said that on the way home they were saying how they'll get me before school's out."

We stopped talking while the waitress put food on the table. The plates were piled high and there was a basket with squares of cornbread and big biscuits.

Tom said the blessing and we were quiet. We pulled silverware from the paper napkins and tasted the food.

"Do you want Tom and me to go to the school to talk to the principal?"

"No, I'll be careful not to be alone where they can get me. I think they'll try on the last day of school because then they'll think they won't get in trouble."

Tom said, "Dayou, promise me you'll call us if you need help."

"I will."

The waitress brought more iced tea. I opened a package of Sweet-n-Low and sifted the powder into my glass. I stirred the ice cubes thinking about how much I hate for kids to be afraid at school. Some of the Columbine emotion edges over into my fear for Dayou. An emotionally disturbed kid, like the boys in

Colorado, could do harm to others who were trying hard to stay straight and do the best they could.

"Why do you think this girl is so unreasonable?" I asked.

"She's real bad. I heard that she came to our school because she had to leave another one for getting into so much trouble. Do you remember that black lady who was shot last year, the one who had some foster children?"

"You mean the one who was a community leader?"

"Yes, that's her. The papers said everybody loved her a lot. This girl is white, but that lady was her foster mother."

"Oh, she's had a terrible year. Maybe she's acting up because of what she's been through."

"Yeah, probably so." Dayou shrugged while she played with her food.

"But, we can't let her hurt you no matter what's going on with her," I said.

"Well, you see why I wish I didn't have to go back to school. I might have my friend turn on a tape recorder on the bus if they keep making threats. That girl denies everything. I would have to have evidence to prove what I know is true."

Dayou had eaten only a few bites. We asked the waitress for a take-out box and began gathering pocketbooks and papers and slipping to the end of the seats.

As we slammed car doors, I wished high school was easier for kids. People who didn't know the inside thought it was carefree and the best time of life, while lots of students struggled to be safe and survive one day at the time. Even if their physical survival was not threatened, their emotional stability was on edge.

22

NEW JOB

Pictures from Home

My fingers shake,
I open the brown envelope,
study Mother's face.
She sits with my brothers, sisters,
cousins, close family
I can't recognize.

In Midtown Square, Tom went to look at books and Dayou took the lead into the shoe store. She moved quickly, as teenagers do, rejecting whole aisles with a glance. She had specified that she wanted black. Her prom dress was mauve.

I walked behind her thinking that we only had forty minutes to get shoes, buy her something for supper and get her to Harris Teeter to start job training at five. She had been hired at the store near her apartment.

It was good to see her doing such a normal teenage thing as shopping for shoes and rushing to a job. Her health and the question of graduation receded a little like distant mountains.

We squeezed down aisles where boxes were stacked on the floor, some with tissue paper spilling out and tops not quite on.

She wanted to come to Burlington Shoes because one of her friends had found her shoes there.

A saleslady moved in our direction. She had light brown skin, wore big glasses and had her hair pulled back. She looked from Dayou to me, and I knew she was wondering what our connection could be. I was surprised that no one ever asked, but the question was always in their faces.

Dayou spotted a pair she liked. "Do you have these in black?" she asked. The lady went into the storage room looking for a size eight and a half.

I glanced at my watch. Dayou applied for this job last year and now that she finally had it, I didn't want her to be late.

She was trying the shoe on her right foot. It was white leather with a clunky high heel and silver strap across the top. She stood and walked to the mirror with her tennis shoe still on the left foot, turning to the side so she could get the full effect.

The clerk came back and said, "You go, girl! That looks good."

Dayou was grinning and I knew these were the ones. The clerk told us they did not have this shoe in black. Dayou wanted to know if they could be dyed. The lady showed her the satin-like shoes that could take dye but explained that the process wouldn't work on leather.

I assured Dayou that white would look fine with her dress, and we moved to the counter to pay. While we waited our turn, she spotted a dot of glue on the strap. She asked for another pair but found out these were the only ones in her size. She approached the manager to ask if he knew how to remove the glue.

He pulled out a cloth and began rubbing. I glanced at my watch every ten seconds. He searched for another solvent at the back of the store.

We were at the front of the line so I pulled out my Visa to pay. Finally, the manager walked up with the shoe. Dayou inspected the strap and said she saw a small scratch. He acknowledged that there was a detectable spot.

She asked, "Then can I get a discount?"

He said, "Of course."

We had to wait our turn again. It was almost four-thirty by then, and I watched the cashier checking out customers as if everything were slowed to the speed of a dream sequence. Dayou said, "Don't worry, I don't need anything to eat."

"Yes, you do," I said. You'll be in there until nine thirty, and I know you haven't eaten today.

"No, but I'm okay."

The lady took my card and began punching in a long line of numbers. She said we would get nine dollars and thirty-eight cents off the price. Dayou looked pleased, and I just wanted the lady to finish. She asked for my address and phone number and then I had to sign the receipt.

I ran to the bookstore to get Tom while the clerk put the shoes in a bag.

At the food court, the lady was busy at the back and seemed mad that customers had interrupted her.

Dayou was not excited over anything on the menu. As she read the board over the window, I asked her to make a quick decision. A choice was made, but when the lady lifted an ice cream scoop filled with chicken salad and dumped it on the bread, I heard Dayou say, "Uhh." I knew she wouldn't eat it. But it was too late to cancel, so we added a drink and a chocolate-chip cookie.

As we moved into thick traffic, I heard paper rattling in the back as she unwrapped the cookie. "I'll eat the sandwich later."

I did my mother thing and warned her not to eat unrefrigerated chicken and mayonnaise. Handing Dayou my cell phone, I asked her to call the manager who hired her and get more specific directions. She always remembered phone numbers so she soon had him on the line. He told her the training center was in a Harris Teeter store on Providence Road. Tom was familiar with the location, so we kept moving as fast as we could.

I went in with Dayou to check on the city bus stop and the schedule. There was a room filled with people in green knit shirts bent over tables reading or writing. The teacher walked to us when we opened the door. She assured us Dayou would be out in time to catch the nine-thirty bus. She said others would be walking to the stop with her.

Tom and I drove out of the parking lot wondering what would happen if she missed the last bus.

* * *

On Thursday, I called to see if Dayou got home okay. She said, "I called a friend when we had break, and she and her boy friend picked me up."

"Do you know which bus to catch this afternoon?" She said she did and would be leaving in ten minutes to walk to the stop.

A few minutes later when I got back from the grocery store, the message light was blinking on the answering machine. Dayou's voice was choked as she said, "My aunt sent pictures of my mother and my brothers and sisters. I just found them in the mailbox."

As I listened to her voice, I looked at the picture of my family taken at Thanksgiving. It stood on a shelf near the phone. Nine of us had lined up on the front steps between two columns. My son held two-year-old Caroline and my daughter had two-month-old Troy. We'd brought out cameras before the first ones had to leave. I studied their faces as Dayou talked and thought how much I loved each one.

"My mom looks so sad," Dayou said. "She's so small now." There was a pause and she said, "I'll talk to you later, when I have a break tonight." I could hear the tears in her voice. This was her first look at her mother in eight years.

At nine she called back. Her voice still trembled. "Mrs. Noell, my mom is so small. She is not nearly as big as she used to be. She is skinny."

"Are you afraid she's not getting enough to eat?"

"Yes, I remember her being a large woman. There are five children standing around her and a baby on her lap. I don't know who some of them are. I don't like the way the children are dressed. I want to start working so I can send some money for food and mail a package of clothes."

I glanced at the photograph of my family again. They were content after a turkey dinner.

"I'm sorry you are so worried, but I am glad you got the pictures."

"Me, too. My aunt also mailed a photograph of her sister who's in this country. I think it's an old picture. My mom sent two African dresses. I wonder if she made them herself. I hope they fit. I want to wear one of them to church Sunday, and I'm going to take the pictures so I can show everybody."

We said goodbye and I regretted that I wouldn't be able to see the pictures for two weeks. Tom and I were headed on vacation to Germany, Austria and Switzerland.

23

PICTURES

My Uncle James

Coughs, wheezes
day and night.
I don't know how to help.
They sent him home
from work on Tuesday.

Tom and I returned from Europe on Tuesday night. I had thought about Dayou and the pictures when we saw the Passion Play at Oberramegau, when we rode up the cog-wheel railway to see the Matterhorn and in the shops of Lucerne where we bought her a tee-shirt.

She called Wednesday and asked about our trip. She said she was worried about her uncle. "He's coughing all the time, and I don't know what to do for him."

"Has he been to the doctor?" I asked. She said he went a few days ago, but she didn't know if that trip had been to get help with his breathing problem or arthritis.

I asked if he was on prescription medication. She said some of it did not have a pharmacy number, so I wondered if he was using over-the-counter meds.

I told her we'd stop by.

* * *

We climbed the metal steps to the second story apartment. The units were built about fifty years ago, but fairly well maintained. We knocked on the door, thick with dark brown paint.

Dayou was smiling when she let us in through the kitchen. Something was cooking in a pot on the stove. We walked into the living room which had two sofas and several chairs all covered with throws. James bought these pieces used when he came to Charlotte in 1992. An artificial flower arrangement sat on the coffee table with some medicine bottles and a few bills. The TV was against the wall next to the kitchen door.

James was sitting slightly bent over as if he could breathe better in that position.

"James, how are you feeling?" I asked.

"Not well," he said. "I'm having a bad time with asthma."

Tom sat on the sofa. I stood in front of James so I would not miss any of his words. I didn't want him to have to repeat. Every breath was hard work.

"You remember I told you I had a bad time with asthma during the war in Liberia? That time I got so weak I couldn't walk."

"Yes, I recall hearing you tell Tom about that when Dayou was in the hospital."

"Well, this is not that bad, but I'm having trouble working. Tuesday I got so sick they sent me home."

"Can you take some sick leave?"

"I could. I have three weeks and a few vacation days. But if I use it all, I don't know what will happen if I get worse later on."

"Did you go to the doctor?"

"Yes, but I don't think the medicine he gave me is helping. I have called the office, but he can't see me until next Tuesday. They will be closed for Memorial Day."

138

I looked on the coffee table at his medicine bottles. He had Celebrex, an inhaler and some Ginseng tablets.

"Celebrex is for arthritis. I'm having trouble with that, too."

"I'm glad you are going back to the doctor. There may be something else he can give you."

"I don't know what's going to happen if I can't work. America is a wonderful place, but when bills are due, nobody gives you any consideration because you have been sick. The rent, phone, and utility bills have to be paid, whether you are able to work or not. If I don't get better, I'll have to go back to Liberia. I could probably live there on my 401K, which I started when I worked for the Voice of America."

"Will you get your citizenship before you go?" I asked.

"I have turned in my application. I'm just waiting for them to call to tell me when to take the test. I do want to get that because nobody knows what the future will bring. I might need to come back if fighting breaks out again."

Tom asked Dayou what she was cooking.

She smiled and said, "This is the fufu I told you about. People in Liberia eat this all the time."

Dayou brought the pan into the living room to show my husband the consistency and color, which was similar to biscuit dough.

"You remember I told you my mother grows cassava and grinds it into powder. This is what we make with it."

I knew she was preparing this for James because she didn't eat it. I was glad she was trying to help him.

I walked into the kitchen. "Where are the pictures?" I asked.

"Right here." She picked up two photos from the table.

"This is my mother," she said, touching the woman in the center of the first picture.

"Oh, she looks nice, and who are the children?" They seemed to range in age from a baby to a boy about ten or eleven.

Touching faces, she said, "These three are my half-sisters, and the baby on her lap is my half-brother. I don't know who the others are. Maybe cousins."

We bent our heads over the pictures in front of the sink where the light was best. The photos were in color and of excellent quality. One little boy wore tennis shoes; the others had on flip-flops. Their clothes looked okay and they appeared healthy. They were alert and bright-eyed. Dayou's mother was not smiling, but she looked pleasant, slender but not skinny. Her hair was covered with a piece of tan cloth.

Dayou's mother, Sangay Briggs, with her children and other family members.

"My mom looks so much smaller that I remember her. She has lost a lot of weight."

"That may be, Dayou, but look at her neck area. If she were undernourished, I think the bones would be more prominent. I think she looks good."

Dayou had told me on the phone that her mom looked so sad it made her cry. I didn't think she looked sad as much as stoic, like a woman who had given birth to many children and lost half of them, a woman who had worked hard on her farm and faced the uncertainty of war for ten years. She appeared to be resigned to her life and yet to still have much strength.

I looked back and forth between her face and Dayou's. "I see some favor, Dayou."

"I think I'm a little like her but more like my dad." Dayou touched the baby on her mother's lap. "Isn't he the cutest little boy? He's my favorite already."

"Is the boy standing in the back the one who was a toddler when you left home?"

"I think it could be, but I don't know. I loved him so much, and now I can't even recognize his picture."

"Did you see this one of my aunt?"

I turned back to the table. The brown envelope was addressed to Layee Kolo.

"Dayou, your aunt put your real name on here."

"Yes, that's it, Layee."

She pulled out an eight-by-ten photograph. It was old and some of the surface had flecked off. Smiling through all the folds and scratches was a lovely black woman, her hair in soft curls.

"This is my mother's sister who is somewhere in this country. My family wants me to find her. They haven't had a letter in years. The last time they heard, she was living in the Baltimore area. I tried People Search on the internet, but I didn't pick up anything."

"I bet the problem is that you don't know her married name," I said. "Are you searching for Briggs?"

"Yes."

"To locate her is almost impossible unless you have more information."

"I'm so glad you got the pictures. It's sad to think about the girl who was bringing the first set when her plane went down off Ivory Coast."

We were silent bending over the pictures. I was thinking about how important this was to Dayou, bigger than Christmas, her birthday or any other special day. I knew she had studied her mother's face over and over during the past two weeks.

"I'm glad your aunt had a duplicate set," I said, straightening up. "I wish we had some of your dad."

"I'm going to ask my aunt to take some of him. My dad is getting to be an old man. I hope I can see him again – maybe next year." She carefully slid the photographs into the brown mailer and closed the flap.

"Do you want me to pick you up Sunday?"

"Yes, and I'll have on one of the dresses my mother sent me. I'll wear the purple one. Purple is my favorite color."

I went back into the living room to speak to James and to pick up my pocketbook. He and Tom were talking.

"James, we are planning a party for Dayou when she graduates. We want you to come. Do you think you can? It will either be on June second or third," I said.

"I would certainly like to if I feel well enough."

"You know we live in Davidson, which is about twenty-five miles up I-77, but maybe I can work out a ride for you so you won't have to drive."

"That would be good. I would appreciate it. I'd like to come."

"You have done so much for Dayou. You, of all people, need to come."

142

Tom, Dayou and I clicked down the metal steps to the car. James followed, being the good host.

"If I go back to Liberia, she can have this furniture. Then she could get an apartment and not have to buy anything to get started."

I wondered how James could manage in Liberia. I had read on the internet that services were limited, so I thought it might be hard or impossible for him to get his medicines. His children and grandchildren would need the money he had. Tuition had to be paid for the kids' schooling and unemployment was high. One of his daughters was starting a school. I had seen pictures and I knew there were lots of needs, and money could disappear quickly.

I also worried that Dayou would not be able to afford an apartment on her own.

"Giving her the furniture would be nice," I said, "very nice. I hope you will feel much better. Please do see the doctor on Tuesday. Dayou has been worried about you."

"Yes, I will."

James and Tom shook hands as Dayou and I got into the car.

24

CASSANDRA DRAKEFORD

Mrs. Drakeford

*Cheerleader sponsor,
rescuer, hair styler,
friend.*

Dayou gave me the phone number of Ms. Drakeford and I called to set up a time we could talk. She had been such an important person in Dayou's life, and I wanted to hear her account. She was happy to tell me about their relationship, but suggested we do it over the phone because of her busy schedule.

She told me about meeting Dayou at Piedmont Middle School when Dayou entered seventh grade, and how Dayou struggled. Her English was hard to understand. Her speech was rapid, with words running together, and she did not enunciate clearly. Ms. Drakeford said kids made fun of the way Dayou talked.

Ms. Drakeford said Dayou's clothes were not stylish, and she was having trouble fixing her hair. She came by the guidance office when problems popped up or when she needed a little reassurance. She worked hard on her schoolwork, but Ms. Drakeford said, "I felt she needed something extra."

"Since I was the cheerleader sponsor, I suggested Dayou try out for the squad in eighth grade. All her teachers signed the forms, and she did a good job with the cheers. After she was selected, some of the girls said, 'How can she do this when we can hardly understand her speech?'"

"But," Ms. Drakeford said, "she did well and was such a support to me. If some of the girls were pouty and had an attitude, Dayou talked to them. She said, 'Mrs. Drakeford gives her time to help us, and you need to shape up and do your best for her.' Amazingly, they listened to her and the problem was solved."

"During this time she began to dress better. I don't know if someone was taking her shopping, but her clothes were like what the other kids were wearing. I asked her one day if she would like me to show her how to fix her hair. Her face brightened and she said, 'Would you do that for me?' I took her home after school, washed her hair and did a style where her hair was pulled up and fastened in the back. She loved it. In fact that style is the one she has in the cheerleading pictures, and if you come to my house, you'll see that picture on my wall."

The teachers encouraged Dayou. When some of the girls got pregnant and dropped out of school, Dayou rose above her problems and showed a lot of strength. One of the encouragers was Tony Dula, her English as a Second Language teacher.

Ms. Drakeford told me that she transferred to the office at West Charlotte High when Dayou entered there in the ninth grade and that she remembered that Dayou was very close to David Butler, her math teacher.

"The house fire that killed him hurt all of us," she said. "His sister is a friend of mine. We were crushed. The key had melted in the dead bolt and he died from smoke inhalation. Dayou suffered. David might have been a little like a father image to her."

"Let me give you an example of Dayou's independent spirit. One day in the tenth grade some students left a mess on a cafeteria table. Dayou had sat there but she had not been guilty. Mrs. Lockhart, an assistant principal, asked Dayou to clean it up. Dayou said, 'I will this time.' She didn't care for Mrs. Lockhart after that."

"When Dayou returned to school after her surgery, her grades were messed up. Apparently, the grades had not come in from the teacher for homebound, or more likely had been misplaced, and Dayou received all F's. She was so upset. She came to me and I took her to Mrs. Lockhart."

"Mrs. Lockhart said, 'Dayou, if I get this fixed for you, will you like me again?' Dayou's reply was, 'I don't know.'"

I asked about the problems Dayou had shortly before graduation.

"There were some bad times in the twelfth grade," Ms. Drakeford said. "Dayou came to me telling about a girl who had threatened to beat her up. The girl was in her face and would not stop. I got so angry. Dayou did not want to go down to her level. She wanted to graduate without problems, but she worried about her safety," Ms, Drakeford continued. "I called the police officer assigned to the school. I said, 'You need to handle this situation, or I'm going to do something myself that might cause me to lose my job.'"

"The girl seemed to get her anger under control before the end of the school year, and she did not try to fight."

"Dayou had a run-in with the French teacher. That was when Dayou needed a tissue and the teacher wouldn't let her go to the bathroom. Dayou had never asked before. The teacher said, 'No,' but Dayou went anyway because she didn't know what else to do. The teacher called the resource officer and said a student was out of control. She locked the door and Dayou couldn't get back in. Dayou was suspended three days."

"I tried to talk to the teacher and tell her that if she knew Dayou better, she would see this in a different way. At the end of school, she came into my office and said, 'I misjudged your baby.'"

Ms. Drakeford closed the conversation with comments about Dayou's strength. "Even though she is strong," she said, "I know she wants people to realize that she is human too. She needs mothering and love just as we all do. I tried to give her a little bit of that."

I realized how important this friendship was to Dayou. Cassandra Drakeford was there for her every school day for six years. Dayou knew that she could get help whenever she needed it, whether it was for academic work or personal relationships. Ms. Drakeford gave the kind of support most students receive from parents, and this was a key factor in encouraging Dayou to keep trying.

25

GRADUATION

Graduation Guests

I want
my father here,
white African shirt, carved cane –
my mother, wrapped in colors
with matching headpiece.

I want to feel
their proud smiles on this June night.

June 1, 2000

We walked across the parking lot in hot, still air. Families
squeezed out of cars, stepping onto black asphalt, straightening
their best clothes. Grandmothers walked slowly. Little kids
bounced ahead while parents cautioned them to wait.

If Dayou's parents could be here for graduation, her mother
would be wearing an African dress in vivid colors complimenting
her brown skin with matching material wrapped and tied for her
headpiece. Her shoes would be black leather slippers. Her father
would walk slowly in a white African shirt with the round, black
hat on his head. With his right hand, he'd carry a carved, wooden

149

cane. What would they think of the big roundness of the Charlotte Coliseum with cars stretching out from it like a huge intricate rug?

As we approached the turnstiles, I realized the tightness of security. A lady searched my bag and inspected Tom's camera.

We found seats and looked at the people around us. Some were dressed conservatively; others had baggy shorts, huge tee shirts and tennis shoes without socks. Some of the girls wore low neck blouses and short skirts, and they moved around constantly greeting friends or trying to get a better view.

At eight thirty, the band began playing "Pomp and Circumstance," and the crowd cheered and applauded as the seniors, accompanied by the marshals, marched in. We knew Dayou was positioned near the end, so we waited before trying to spot her. Tom had his binoculars and after a while he said, "Here she comes. She has sprayed her hair with the copper color we saw kids in Europe wearing. She'll be easy to spot."

Her parents would like the marching. In Liberia, every village has musicians who play during celebrations.

Dayou missed passing her math competency test by one point. She immediately said, "I'm taking a review class this summer, and then I'll take the exam again. I'm determined to get my diploma. I've come too far not to graduate. They'll let me walk across the stage on June 1, but I'll get an attendance certificate."

I took off my glasses and focused the binoculars to search for her. I was excited that she was at this point; yet, I wanted her to have the greater satisfaction of the diploma. I knew how many times she'd wanted to give up.

I saw the copper hair pulled into a pony tail. Only the back was sprayed. She looked happy as the maroon tassel swung on her mortarboard.

Tom looked again. "There's somebody she knows on the other side," he said. "She's waving, but I can't see who it is."

I thought it might be Debra. She had always told Dayou there would be lots of people from our church at her graduation, but Debra's sister died last week and Debra didn't feel up to organizing a group to come.

Tom and I had decided to give a dinner party at our house in Davidson tomorrow night. I had asked Dayou to give me the names of some friends she would like to invite. Graduation ceremonies in Charlotte extend over two days, so I knew some would be involved on Friday and unable to come. I had already talked to the members of the team that cared for her after surgery, and they were going to help with food.

The seniors settled into chairs on the basketball floor and the music and speeches began. The last of the student presenters was the valedictorian, Sheldon Holliday Welton. She spoke about how she and her classmates benefited from attending a diverse school. Welton referred to the recent court decision to go from cross-town busing to neighborhood schools. She felt this would short change students who really needed to learn to value all people.

Tom and I noticed the racial make-up of the class. We guessed about seventy-five percent were black, twenty percent white and five percent Asian. Tom wondered why we didn't see Hispanic names on the program. West Charlotte has an ESL program (English as a second language), and I would have thought this school would be even more international.

The principal announced that everyone should hold their applause until all graduates had received their diplomas. I knew this was a futile request. The marshals brought the students up to the platform steps in groups. People began yelling and cheering as students' names were called. Fortunately, names were said without pause, so it was impossible to tell which student was getting the applause. Cameras were raised and parents were beaming.

A man stood at the railing below us. He wore a bright blue suit with blue and white shoes. He waited, anticipating the name, then clapped and yelled, calling his son or grandson's name and turned to the rest of us with a satisfied smile.

Some people began to leave while the ceremony was still going on. Tom handed me the binoculars just before Dayou crossed the stage. The woman on his right decided at that moment to leave, and suddenly I was seeing her hips through the lens as she pushed past saying, "Excuse me." I was angry that someone wouldn't wait two minutes when it had to be evident, by my posture that the student I had come to see was on stage. When I refocused on Dayou, she was headed back to her seat, waving the diploma cover and walking triumphantly. Even though I wished this could be the real thing, Dayou was not dwelling on that, but on the idea that she would get it soon. Her survival instincts carried her on.

Would her parents be standing and cheering or clapping with quiet dignity? I knew their smiles would be big. After all, she was only the second one in her family to graduate.

After the last song, Tom went down to the railing near the floor to try to get Dayou's attention. She knew we were planning to be there, but we wanted her to see us. We had offered to bring her, but she said she had to be early so she rode with a friend.

Tom spotted Bill and Lois Bunpus. They said she hadn't seen them either, so as she marched out, Tom called her name and waved his handkerchief. She looked all around and then yelled, "Hey," and her smile spread. The Lolin family from Liberia and Paula Emrich, all from our church, were on the other side waving as she passed.

I thought of another night when she had gone past us. That was two and a half years ago when we waited in the hall to see her rolled out of the operating room. We had all been speechless as the nurses had pushed her silently away and through the swinging doors into recovery. As I replayed that night from two years ago over in my head, I wondered what would happen to Dayou next.

She had wanted to invite the family who had agreed to the liver donation. I had told her we couldn't because they had chosen to remain anonymous. When she asked why, I smiled at her and said I thought that if a person received a vital organ, and didn't do well in life, the family might not want to know.

"Dayou, I know that if they knew you, they'd be proud. But we have to respect their wishes."

26

THE PARTY

Celebration

White tablecloths snapping,
African violets, ferns,
okra, chocolate cake,
friends.

I took white cloths from under plastic laundry covers and shook them over the tables, smoothing down fold wrinkles. The good china went on the long table in the dining room and the second best dishes on two card tables, one to the side in the dining room and the other in the front vestibule. I tied a graduation balloon on the back of Dayou's chair at the end of the big table, folded matching napkins and placed them under forks. I put African violets on the tables and mantels. Our house was a Victorian, so there were mantels in every room. Someone from the Congo once told me that they had never seen an African violet at home, so I wondered if they carried the name but not the point of origin. Even so, I still liked the idea of "African" flowers.

In a box in the garage, I found my son's mortarboard from college and hung it on the mirror in the hall over one of Dayou's senior pictures.

While Tom mowed the grass, I arranged ferns and flowers at the top of the back steps, put a ham in the oven and made tall pitchers of tea. A restaurant was cooking the chicken which we would pick up after five.

I tried to call a few people who hadn't let me know if they were coming. The guest list changed from hour to hour. Originally, we expected three girls from Liberia. Then they said they had to work. I wondered if that were the real reason, or if they wouldn't come because they didn't know me very well and thought they might be uncomfortable.

Mary Ann Joseph from Trinidad, who was in our church, said she was coming. She also graduated last night. I asked Barry Long to drive the van so that anyone who needed a ride could meet him at the church. I hoped James would come, and I didn't know if he'd drive up I-77 in rush hour traffic.

Sometime after six, Dayou called. I heard panic in her voice. "Mrs. Noell, I don't know what to do. My uncle is not here. I have called a cab to take me to church to meet Barry, but it hasn't come." I told her I'd try to get Barry's cell phone number and ask him to come by her apartment. I reassured her that he would not leave town without her. I was beginning to wonder if this party was going to fall apart. Dayou immediately called back saying Barry was at her place.

Lois and Bill came a little early because she had cooked several dishes and had said she would help with last-minute preparations. We began arranging food on an extra table in the kitchen and getting out serving spoons. While we were working, Barry, Randy Williams, Dayou and a friend of hers came in the back door. I greeted everybody and invited them into the living room.

Dayou didn't introduce the girl with her. Her face was familiar, and I remembered that I had taken her and Dayou to the library one Saturday to work on a project and that she was from

156

Nigeria. Her dad taught at UNCC and was a poet. Her name escaped me. She told me it was Amregae and that she, too, graduated from West Charlotte last night.

I heard Carol Harlan's voice at the back, so I went to open the door carrying a handful of silverware. She and Dale brought Mary Ann and her sister Gail who was in college in Pennsylvania. Dale carried a big pot of green beans to the stove. The girls all gathered on the sofa in the vestibule. I was watching bread in the oven while Lois filled glasses with ice. We quickly set two more places for Gail and Amregae. I was so pleased they had come since Dayou's other friends couldn't make it.

Jane, Barry's wife, arrived with her daughter Joanna who was a little younger than Dayou and her son Benjamin who was twelve. Bobbi Williams, who came with them, carefully carried the graduation cake which was decorated with mortarboards and ribbons.

The women were reheating food and pulling out more serving pieces. I have always loved this time when the house is clean, the tables ready, the cooking finished and everybody talks in groups all over the downstairs, anticipating the meal.

Dayou smiled as she came to tell me how much she liked our house. This was the first time she had been to Davidson. I knew she was pleased to be the center of attention and to feel the warmth of these people. All the adults present and some of the teenagers formed a wall of protection around her during surgery, recovery and the solving of regular problems. Last month, Barry and Joanna even helped her do a power-point presentation for her senior exit project.

So many times when other teenagers went home to family, Dayou went home to an empty apartment. Tonight was different.

I asked Tom to call everybody to the kitchen. As people moved into the room, we stood in a large semi-circle. I asked Dayou to introduce her friends. We all knew Mary Ann but not

157

Gail or Amregae. I suggested the young people sit with Dayou at the big table.

Dale prayed. He thanked God for Dayou's life and asked a special blessing on her as she "goes down new, unexplored roads."

I looked around at the different faces, wishing James were here. He was the reason she was able to leave Liberia, and he had supported her for seven years. I wondered why he didn't come. He was at our daughter's wedding reception. Why was he not here, now?

I also missed Debra. She had been such a big part of Dayou's life.

We began the serving line with Dayou in front. I had told her we would have chicken, since that was a favorite of hers. She said, "I want fried okra," and Tom picked it up at the restaurant. She was a picky eater, but tonight she filled her plate and carried a glass of iced tea to the table.

During dinner, I listened to heavy southern accents from the Carolinas and Kentucky. The singing rhythms of Trinidad mixed with the touch of British in Nigerian speech and the tribal rhythms from Liberia. As the sounds washed over me, I felt content that we were together, laughing, teasing, telling our stories. I thought how this same group would probably never share a meal again, but we would enjoy tonight.

27

THE PARTY WENT ON

I Remember When...

Mr. Bumpus called people to pray,
Mrs. Bumpus and Mrs. Noell
stayed all night at the hospital,
I slept on the couch at Bobbi's.
Every day,
arms have been around me,
holding on.

Dayou, Mary Ann and Gail sat on the 1800's sofa in our house. The carved sides formed beautiful rounded lines. I thought about the original owners who lived during the aftermath of the Civil War, and somehow I wanted them to know these girls were entertained as guests on the sofa.

We added dining chairs until there were fourteen seats in the living room. Carol and Dale Harlan left early to attend a wake.

As people moved into the room, Bobbi discovered Tom's supply of cinnamon hot balls and said, even though they were not on the menu, she couldn't resist. Mary Ann asked what they were, and we offered her one. She was quiet for a minute and then began to fan her mouth with her hand and make faces. Some of the other kids took one, and we laughed at their expressions of

159

pain. Finally, I got up and brought Mary Ann a glass of ice water. Experienced eaters knew to keep the wrapper, so they could take a break. Mary Ann asked if she could take one home for her father. We insisted she take two so her mother could enjoy one, too.

After this teasing and laughing, I suggested, since all of us had a history with Dayou, that we tell some of our memories. Again, I missed James and Debra because I would have liked for them to add their stories and hear what others had to say.

Bobbi Williams talked first. She was in her forties and had an endless supply of energy.

Bobbi and Randy's son Drew, who was now seventeen, had just finished the eleventh grade. He couldn't be with us tonight because he was the photographer for graduation at his school.

"I remember the night of the transplant," Bobbi began. "We didn't know where Dayou was going after she left the hospital, so I said, 'I'll be at work Monday through Friday, but if you can arrange care, she can come to my house.' Debra, Lois and Carolyn sat there working out schedules."

Randy said, "When Bobbi told me the plan, I started thinking what had to be done. I knew I could move her furniture on my truck. I thought she would be in her room a lot so I had cable run in. I don't think she ever stayed one whole night in there. She slept in the den on the couch for two months."

Dayou laughed, "That's true. I didn't sleep in the bedroom. The cable was never used, and I only went in there to get dressed."

Randy leaned back in his chair with his arms crossed.

Barry and Jane Long were close friends of Bobbi and Randy. Barry, a computer engineer for Duke Power, sat in a wingback beside the hearth with an antique lamp casting soft shadows as he reminisced. Barry taught the Sunday school class Dayou attended, visited her in the hospital and was always a great support person. He stretched long legs crossing them at the ankles.

"Dayou, I'll never forget the night we met at the church to pray for you," Barry said. "Bill Bumpus called all the deacons and asked us to come. I left there feeling that whatever happened was in God's control."

Jane sat next to Barry in a straight chair. She was a tall, attractive woman in her forties who taught pre-school. She told us about the Charlotte Leadership Forum that she and Barry belonged to three years ago.

"We were talking about Dayou to some members. One of them was a doctor at Carolina's Medical. He was upset that nothing was being done at that time to push for the transplant. Later, he told us that he had talked with other doctors involved with the case and told them that he didn't know other people at the church, but he did know Barry and me and that he felt we were reliable people. He said, 'If these people tell you they will be responsible for after-care, they will do it.'"

I had never heard this before. I found it interesting that after knowing Jane and Barry such a short time, this man had made such a correct assessment.

Lois said, "I remember the nights Carolyn and I stayed with you at the hospital, Dayou. One night, she was there until one or two in the morning and then I came in. One night when I got there, Carolyn was worried because you had gotten up to go to the bathroom and didn't know where you were. We knew you were really sick by then."

Joanna told about going on a youth retreat when she and Dayou were roommates and what a good time they'd had laughing and talking into the night.

Words circled the room. "I remember...."

"Don't forget the time...."

"Do you remember when?"

161

As remembrances wound down, I added, "Dayou and I are writing about her life. On Wednesday afternoons, when we were driving to the doctor's office, having supper together or after homework was finished, she talked about Africa and I asked questions. You all know about how she almost lost her life due to hepatitis. I want to read the section we wrote about another time she was in danger in Liberia. This was when Charles Taylor, who led the rebel troops, came into Monrovia and Dayou and her sister's family escaped." I read the chapter to the group.

Joanna asked, "Would your father be like our mayor?"

"Yes, similar," Dayou said. "He had a house in each of his villages and one in Totota."

"Do you think his life was in danger?"

"We didn't know. So many people were being tortured or shot that there was no way to know. My brother did fight with Charles Taylor, and that may have kept my family safe."

Jane said, "Tell us about your mother."

"She farms land that belonged to her father. She is a strong woman and works hard. I helped when I lived with her. We grew rice, yams, okra, peppers and a plant you don't know called cassava."

Gail asked, "How long has it been since you saw your parents?'

"I was eleven when I left home. I was in Ivory Coast a year and a half before coming here."

"Do you have brothers and sisters?"

"Yes, I have half-brothers and sisters, but I am the only one left of the children my parents had together."

As the questions continued, I realized this was the first time most of them had heard much about Dayou's life in Liberia.

Tom asked her to tell what she had heard from home.

"My family all survived the fighting but there are no jobs. Clinics and schools were messed up by the rebels. Some kids go to class without a roof over their heads. A million people left home because of the war and lots of them will never go back. The Lutheran missionaries in Totota stayed, but most left. The U.N. does give out rice. I saw pictures of Monrovia. It breaks my heart to see how much of it was torn up. It was a beautiful town. Charles Taylor was our hope, but now he doesn't seem to care about the people – only about getting rich."

The group was quiet, trying to imagine living where the places they loved were so changed.

About nine-thirty, some of the women stood, knowing they needed to pack up food.

After some left, I went back into the living room to find Barry, Randy, Tom and the girls still talking. Barry offered to take Mary Ann and Gail home since Dale and Carol left early. On the drive back they'd be with Dayou and Amregae.

After the last good-byes, I sank down on the built-in seat in the kitchen. I was exhausted but pleased the party had gone so well. I knew the other kids had family celebrations, and I wanted this for Dayou. These people were her family.

Tom was running water to wash the china. I saw bubbles over the edge of the sink as I reached for the drying cloth. Images of Liberia edged into my mind. I felt the sadness of people trying to hold onto hope. So many had been killed, injured or displaced to get a man into power who cares only for his personal wealth and who walks on the backs of folks who made heavy sacrifices for him. I thought many of them must be waiting for help from us, help that wasn't coming.

Dayou (center) with friends Mary and Gail at the party given at the Noell's house after graduation, June 2000.

28

THE DIPLOMA

The Party, If I Were Home

Daddy's wives stir cooking pots,
half-sisters chop fruit,
boys run with invitations.
Drummers arrive
at dusk.

At church the next day, Dayou wore a beige flowered skirt with a beige blouse. Her hair was braided and pulled back. She stood with hands in the air like a successful politician on election night, her smile confident as she stepped up to the podium.

The youth minister introduced each graduate and asked them to say something about their plans. When it was Dayou's turn, she said, "I will go to Central Piedmont Community College this fall. My goal is to go into nursing."

The congregation applauded. Those who had known Dayou for the past five years smiled as they turned to look at each other.

I thought of the ones who had often asked about her. Some, like white-haired Velma Rallings, had slipped twenty dollars into my hand on Sunday mornings for her lunch money; others had cornered me in the hall in December, asking for Christmas present suggestions. They were the same folks who, this month, asked for graduation gift ideas.

They didn't know much about her life in Africa or her daily life now, but they did know she needed people who cared that she had lunch and the right clothes and that she needed someone to hug her and ask how she was.

Dayou moved back to her seat. I marveled at her obvious pleasure in the moment. My fingers tightened on the hymnbook. I wanted the diploma to be a reality.

* * *

Two weeks later Dayou called to say she had enrolled in the math review class. "Mrs. Noell, the teacher is so good. He is retired, but he came back to teach this summer. If I had had him all along, I could have passed the competency test before now."

"That's great, Dayou," I answered.

We talked about going to Central Piedmont on Wednesday so we could check on registration and placement tests. Arrangements were made to meet at three.

* * *

We parked in the multi-level lot at the community college and started down the sidewalk when a handsome young man stopped to speak to Dayou. She introduced him as Mentor Dahn, the brother of her friend Yoyo.

"Are you from Liberia?" I asked.

"Yes."

"Dayou has taught me a little about your country. Where did you live?"

"In Monrovia. I'm from the Gio tribe and speak their language."

I smiled, nodding as I tried to remember where this group lived. "Is it east of the Kpelle area?"

"Yes, and slightly north. I like knowing where my roots are," he said. "It makes me feel connected to my people."

"I can understand that."

"So, Dayou," Mentor asked, "what are you doing here?"

She tilted her head to one side and grinned. "I'm registering for school. What do you think?"

I asked Mentor what year he was, and he said he had one more semester before he went on to a four-year college to major in architecture.

"I missed one semester because I wrecked my car. Otherwise, I would be out of here by now," he said.

As we moved on to Garinger Hall, I asked, "Didn't Mentor come to see you when you were in the hospital?"

"Yes, he did."

"I thought he looked familiar."

As we walked, I thought about Mentor. He was a bright star that Liberia needed, one of the displaced who would probably never go home. What would an architect do in a country that wasn't building?

Dayou spoke to two girls she knew before we got to the door of the administration building.

In the office, a lady checked on the computer to see that she was in the system.

Dayou said, "I filled out the registration forms in high school."

"They're here," the secretary said, as she peered at the screen. She looked up frowning, "but there is no date filled in for graduation. Is this a mistake?"

"I'm going to summer classes," Dayou said, "and I hope to have my diploma in a few weeks."

At the counselors' office, a receptionist told her she needed an appointment to take placement tests. This was set up for the next morning. Then she would be told which courses to register for. She was reminded that she could not take the courses unless she had a diploma.

We walked back to the car with July heat rising from too much pavement. Dayou was quiet. I wondered if she were afraid to let herself be too happy until she knew what was going to happen.

As she got out of the car at her apartment, I reached for a map of Africa which had fallen to the floor. I looked at the west coast and traced the outline of Liberia. I saw this country on its knees, circled by 250,000 ghosts – those killed since 1988. Thousands more were refugees torn from their homes during the fighting. Liberia had farms and a few market stalls left. Leaders bled it; rain forests were being hauled away on ships.

I wondered if Liberia could be nursed back to health. Could her people have jobs and clinics and textbooks? Did anyone in the world care, and if they did, could they figure out how to help? Would Dayou ever be able to help her own family?

* * *

Friday morning, August 11th, Tom answered the speaker phone upstairs. From the den where I was reading, I could hear someone yelling. I wondered who it was that was making so much noise. Then Tom called, "There's someone who wants to speak to you."

I knew immediately it was Dayou with good news. I picked up the extension in the kitchen.

"Mrs. Noell, I passed, I passed!" she yelled.

"Oh, Dayou, that's wonderful." I was grinning and silently saying, "Thank you, God."

I saw the yellow-lined pad where I had taken so many notes on her memories of Africa. I visualized brilliant flowers, dirt

168

roads, houses with metal roofs and her family gathering around her.

"I'm so happy for you, Dayou. This is great."

"I just called. I thought the school wasn't telling me because I had failed. Now I can go Monday to pick up my diploma. I'm the happiest person in the world."

Dayou deserved happiness. It had been a long road from the first school in Totota and the small class in Ivory Coast to Crown Point Elementary in Charlotte, Piedmont Middle and finally West Charlotte High. The diploma was hers even though she missed most of the early grades when basic skills were introduced.

Who else would she call? I wished she could share this with her parents. I wondered what they would say or do.

I asked, "Dayou, if you were home, would there be a party similar to the one we had here at our house?"

"Oh, yes. There would be a party."

"Tell me about it. Would it be at your mother's farm?"

"No, not there. It would be in Totota, either at my aunt's or at my dad's. Probably at my dad's house."

"Would your mother go there?"

"Oh, sure. That would not be a problem. My mom wouldn't miss it. She'd be proud of me."

"Tell me what would happen if you were in Africa today."

"Well, first, my dad would send word by his young sons that there would be a feast tonight to honor his daughter – Layee Tume Kolo, the high school graduate."

"My mom and aunts would cook all day and carry food to my father's house in Totota. His other wives would bend over their cooking pots, stirring, while some would cut fruits and vegetables."

"At dusk drummers would come in and start the music."

As Dayou talked, I imagined the scene: flashes of color on the roads as the women walked. Children ran ahead, squealing, mama warnings floating over their heads. The men came talking quietly.

"Tell me who would be there."

"Half-brothers and sisters, their wives and husbands, children, aunts, uncles and cousins would come. Close friends would be in the crowd which would be well over a hundred."

"As soon as everybody is present, the meal would begin. After having spinach soup, everybody would fill their plates with roasted meat, rice, fu-fu and beans. For desert, we would eat cut-up plums, oranges and pineapples."

"After supper, we would begin singing to the drum beats. We'd have a great time."

As Dayou talked, I imagined Sangay Briggs, a woman too independent to be the chief's wife for long, as she watched this daughter from a distance, a daughter who didn't stay with the tribe, marry young and have children as the others were doing. But, then, she always said she wouldn't. As a little girl she was strong willed and said she would go to America.

I saw Nylia Kolo, the medicine man, smiling as he leaned on his carved cane, his white shirt bright against the night, watching his daughter sway into the rhythm, singing, clapping and dancing as an African woman.

29

PICTURES AND WORDS FROM HOME

Audiotape from Totota

*I hear the deepness of
my father's voice.
He's building a house,
wants a new bed.
I'll wire the money.*

December 2001

Red tail lights stretched ahead of us in early evening dark. Dayou and I sat still or slowly inched forward in the mix of going-home traffic and Christmas shoppers. It was unusual for us to have an evening together. Last year she went to the community college and worked at Harris Teeter in the evenings and on weekends. This year she worked full-time at a day care and was not enrolled in school.

"Tom left the picture of your Aunt Meatta crossing the St. Paul River at Quality Chrome to have a slide made," I said. "We will have it on the screen at the front of the church on the sixteenth."

"I love that picture of her in what looks like a canoe made from a burned out log," I said.

"I'll tell her when we talk again that she was in front of the whole church," said Dayou. "She'll like that 'cause she loves church. In fact, she was crossing the river to preach."

"Yeah, I saw she had written that on the back."

"Mrs. Bumpus is working hard on the program for the sixteenth. Someone from each country will carry their flag, and Mrs. Epps will play their national anthems as they walk down the aisle. There'll be people from Argentina, Mexico, Jamaica, The Bahamas, Trinidad, Congo and your Liberian folks. Martha Ajawan will lead the ones from your country in singing your anthem."

Meatta Briggs, Dayou's aunt, (second from left) crossing the St. Paul River to preach, March 2001.

Dayou traced the seam in the upholstery with her finger. "I think I'll wear one of the dresses my mother made."

"That's a good idea. I can't wait to see what Martha wears. She looks like an African queen when she comes in on Sunday morning with one of her outfits. The men will be dressed up, too. Amelio Lolin and Charles Browne will have on their decorated shirts."

I reached for an envelope on the floor. "Here are the rest of your pictures. I made some copies at CVS."

Dayou pulled them out and looked at the one of her mother with young children.

"I'm going to ask my aunt to tell me their names. She's never done that." Continuing to study the photograph, she said, "Mrs. Noell, is there a way you can have your picture put into one that's already made?"

"Someone who knows computer graphics might be able to."

Then I understood why she was asking. "You want to be in the picture with your family, don't you?"

"Yes, I'd like that."

I pulled ahead as a space opened between me and the car ahead. There were so many things a person missed when being away from family, and I never thought of them all. Here was another, not having pictures of yourself with them. How many times had Dayou looked at photos with friends and seen them with arms around moms, dads, brothers and sisters? Had she envied their broad smiles, their clowning before the camera? I felt tender towards her as I realized this simple request was so important.

"What you could do," I said, "is cut out a picture of yourself showing your head and shoulders and put it behind the cousins who are standing in back of your mother. Then you could take it to the Kodak machine and make a copy. It wouldn't be perfect but you could see yourself in there with your family."

"That's a good idea. I'll try it."

Dayou's brother Peter had sent an audio tape a couple of weeks ago. She heard the voices of her parents and some of her brothers and sisters. They spoke in Kpelle and English.

"Can you understand much?" I asked.

Dayou zipped and unzipped her black shoulder bag as she said, "I know everything my mother's saying."

"I thought you said you had forgotten all of it."

She smiled. "I thought I had, but as soon as I heard my mother, I understood her."

"That's interesting. What about your dad?"

"No, I got a lady to translate for me. He says he is giving me a piece of land. Peter translated part of it. I don't know why he didn't do all of it. Anyway, my dad says he's building a new house, and all he asks from me is a bed. I'm going to send the money."

"How much will he need? Can you find out?"

"I will ask my cousin, and then I'll send the money through Western Union. They pick it up using a code word I tell them."

"Peter asked my father what he wants me to do. My dad said, 'Tell her to finish school.' Then Peter said, 'What after that?' and my dad said, 'Tell her to come home.'"

This bothered me because I knew she wanted to please her dad, and he didn't understand she would never be able to live where modern medicine was not available. His medicine would not be enough for his daughter.

30

THE MEDICINE MAN'S DEATH

Too Late

My father's gone.
I sob, listen
to his taped voice,
rewind, cry again.
I want to see his face,
feel his arms around me.

December 13, 2001

As I came in from my writers' group, dumping my notebook on the seat in the kitchen, Tom came out of the den with tension in his face.

"Dayou called," he said. "She was crying so hard she couldn't tell me what was wrong."

Halfway down the hall, I paused with my coat over my arm. My muscles tightened, my mind raced as I braced for bad news.

"I didn't even know who she was," Tom said. "Finally, she was able to speak and told me her father is dead."

"Oh, no! How did she find out?"

"Her cousin, the one she talks to, called from Monrovia. You may want to call her back because she was so upset I had trouble

175

understanding her. It's only been about ten minutes since she hung up."

"I will," I said, my fingers tracing the rounded head of the coat hanger. "I'm so sorry she didn't get to see him. She told me last week that he was in the hospital, but I knew she had hope he'd get better and be there when she made her dream trip. She has relived their reunion a thousand times."

I dialed Dayou's cell phone number and waited. She answered in a choked voice.

"Dayou, I'm so sorry. When did Sammy call?"

She broke into tears, "While I was on my break at daycare. I was getting ready to turn off my phone and go back to work."

Dayou was sobbing so much that I waited a moment before speaking. "I know how you wanted to see him. This is so hard." Her crying was uncontrollable, and I thought of her alone in the apartment.

"I'm coming down there, okay?"

"Yes, thank you."

"Tom and I will be there in a few minutes."

"Okay."

I began to think about taking flowers and food. The quickest place would be Harris Teeter, so while Tom bought roasted chicken, rolls and a cake, I selected bright flowers that made me think of Africa, large Shasta daisies, purple blooms whose name I didn't know and a white iris for the middle.

I had always dreaded going in where there's been a death. When I was younger, I told myself a card was as good as a visit. But, since people close to me had died, I knew that nothing took the place of a hug and sitting quietly with someone who was hurting.

We carried our offerings up the metal steps, shiny with rain. I knocked on the door and looked at the layers of brown paint while I listened for footsteps crossing the kitchen floor. Dayou opened the door, and I put the flowers on the table before turning to hug her.

"I'm so sorry," I whispered as I put my arms around her. She held on for a long time before she turned to hug Tom. She invited us into the living room, and I stopped to put the chicken in the refrigerator.

There were two sofas. Tom sat on the one across from the door, and I sat down with Dayou on the one to the right. She picked up her small recorder and played the tape of her father's voice. As he spoke, she sobbed and I put my hand on her back. She punched *rewind* and *play* over and over. I heard her older half-brother Peter and her father Nylia Kolo. Peter asked his father questions and they spoke in Kpelle.

"I'm so glad your brother had that tape made, Dayou." I knew it meant everything to hear her father's voice.

She nodded.

After a few minutes, I asked if she knew what caused his death.

"I don't know," she said, "but on the tape, he mentioned he had high blood pressure. My cousin said the doctors at the hospital had not found anything wrong, and some of the medicine men took him out. He also said for the last few days my dad could not speak."

"He may have had a stroke?"

"It sounds as if that could be, and I bet his friends took him off and tried to heal him with country medicine."

We listened to the continual click of the tape player and to her dad's voice. I noticed the clock on the opposite wall with the minute hand sweeping and the hour staying at six o'clock. I wondered how long it had been doing such a miserable job of keeping time. There were three vases of artificial flowers, two on the coffee table. To mourn the life of an African man, I wanted real flowers, bright flowers in the room.

"Dayou, if you don't mind, I'll bring the flowers we brought you in here."

"That'll be fine."

I moved one of the vases to a table next to the wall and brought in the fresh arrangement. The orange daisies and purple blooms looked out of place in the dim room. There were no lights on and the cloudy day was fading into early dark.

Three young women who worked with Dayou at the daycare came in. Dayou introduced them to Tom and me, and they found seats. They told her how sorry they were and we made conversation for a few minutes. Dayou was able to pull herself together to talk to them, and I knew it made her feel good that they came by.

After the brown door closed behind them, Dayou had a phone call. She said very little, listened and then said goodbye and hung up.

"That was the mother of one of my friends," she said.

"In Liberia?"

"No, she lives here. She said, 'I saw ants the other day that had heads like worms. They were not worms, but they had the same heads. I knew somethin' was going to happen when I saw that. They're bad luck. My cousin in Ghana died two days ago and now your dad.'"

I looked at the sweeping minute hand again, the hour still stuck at six o'clock.

Dayou grew calmer. She was more stunned than hysterical, and she began talking more and crying less. She said she was worried about all her father's young children who will not have him to help raise them.

The apartment was growing darker. I wanted to turn on the light, but I wondered if she preferred the dimness. I got up to go into the bathroom, and when I came out, James had come in and the lamp was on. He had just heard the news and was still standing as he reacted to it. He was wearing a dark shirt and light blue jeans with a hole in the knee, which surprised me. I associated jeans with holes with younger people.

"James, did you know her dad?" Tom asked.

"No, I didn't. I'm almost certain I never met him. But I did know some of the Briggs, her mother's family."

"Tell us how they will do the funeral. Do you think they will bury him tomorrow?"

"They may have a wake for two nights, especially since he was a chief. There will be a casket and if the family has the money, they might have him embalmed at a funeral home in Monrovia. Of course, if they don't, the funeral will have to be soon."

I wondered what was happening in all the chief's villages, all the stucco houses with metal roofs. Were the wives crying and wailing, or were they cooking for the wake? How would they live? Was Nylia Kolo still able to provide support for them? What were the children thinking?

Turning to Dayou, James asked, "Are you going to send some money?"

"Yes, I'll talk to my cousin again and make arrangements for it to be picked up. My dad asked me to buy him a bed. Even though he's gone, I'm still going to do it. That's all he asked for – the bed and for me to come home."

31

MOM ON THE PHONE

Mother Calls

I listen to her words,
ache to see her face,
touch her hand.
She says, "Your father
left you land."

I feel like the chief's daughter.

I was reading on the sun porch with January rays pouring
through the wavy glass of our 1905 house when Tom handed me
the phone saying, "It's Dayou."

"Mrs. Noell, I'm so happy; I just talked to my mom." Her
voice rolled on with excitement and joy.

"Were you able to understand each other?"

"Yeah, pretty well. A few times we asked each other over.
Once I was trying to figure out something she said, and she asked
if I was still there because I was quiet. Yeah, we did much better
than before. Remember, then I had to get my brother on the line."

This was the second time Dayou had talked to her mother
since she was eleven. I thought how much lay unsaid between
them, hundreds of hours of explaining, sharing, laughing, sitting

together quietly. Family gossip, friendships, boys, fear during the civil war were all piled up somewhere unspoken. She hadn't told her mother about her first days here, being a cheerleader, getting the award from City Council, surgery and the climb back up. Her mother didn't know Lois, Debra, Bobbi, Tom, me or Dayou's friends. The unsaid was a high mountain to be chipped away piece by piece. Her mom needed to tell, as one adult to another, what had gone on in her life for ten years – go over the births of her children, the deaths of Momi, her mother and Nylia Kola and her dreams for Dayou's future.

"My mom said she has the deed to the land my dad left me, but she said there are problems. Two of my half brothers are trying to get more than their share of everything. One of them is Jackson, who ate the money I sent to share with the family. I told her I want to come in April, but she said I should wait because she is building two houses, one on the farm where she lives and one on my land. She wants me to come after the houses are finished, and then we'll all live together in the house on my land. She said my brothers and sisters are fine and dying to talk to me."

Would Dayou's family feel powerless when they heard the rumors that Charles Taylor might be planning another war – this time with Guinea? What would happen to them and to her if she went back? This fear came on top of the major one about her health. If Dayou were unable to get her meds to keep her from rejecting the liver she received, she would not survive long. She required regular lab work so her doctors could make decisions about medical needs.

"Where was your mother when she called?"

"My cousin Sammy brought her to Monrovia on Thursday, and she's staying with him so she can use the phone. I talked to him a little, too. He is trying to get a scholarship to go to college here. He had heard that he didn't get the one he applied for, so he was disappointed, but he'll try again."

"Is Sammy a good student?"

"Oh, yes, he made excellent grades. He's very smart. The funny thing is that now he talks to me as if I'm on a higher level than he is. I guess it's just because I'm in this country. I don't like it. I want him to talk to me the way he did when we were kids because I've not changed just because I'm here. I miss our old way together."

"Is there a possibility Sammy could go to college in Monrovia? Do you think the colleges are open?"

"I guess they are. You remember they were when we did the research for my senior exit project. I think Sammy just has his heart set on going to school in this country. I hope he can."

Sammy called Dayou often. I wondered if he was hoping she'd find a way to get him here.

"Mom said one of our relatives has a business in Monrovia, so when I want to send something, I can send it to the business and they can pick it up there. It was so good to hear her voice. She says she misses me and can't wait 'til we'll be together."

I watched a male cardinal on the tree outside the sunroom window, wondered if cardinals lived in Africa. They'd be lovely in the rainforest.

"I'm so glad you talked to her, Dayou. That's great, and thanks for calling to tell me about it."

"Okay, I'll see you at church tomorrow, and you know I'm taking my test for citizenship on Monday."

"Oh, that's right. Have you studied the questions?"

"Yes, I think I'm ready. When my uncle got his, he had to wait several months for the ceremony. I have decided that if it comes time to go home, and I don't have my citizenship, I'm going anyway."

Everything about this statement scared me. But Dayou was twenty-one and, as with my own children, I had to sit on the sidelines and watch her call the plays.

32

CITIZEN TUCKER

I am an American citizen

Cameras flash
in front of the flag,
the flag of my
new country.

Dayou showed her paperwork to the guard at the door and she, Lady Dennis and I rushed into the auditorium, moving to seats near the window wall. The décor was government-issue. There were long rows of metal chairs upholstered in gray, arranged primly on gray carpet. The INS official was making opening remarks to an audience resembling the United Nations. On his right, an American flag hung from the ceiling, blocked in stars, stripes descending to the floor.

From the back, I watched the thick, black Asian hair; Scandinavian blonds; black, tight curls of the Africans, and straight Mexican hair. The unifying factor was that everyone wore western clothes. A small Chinese girl on the outside walkway peered in the window, returning my smile.

The official explained that each person would bring his green card and the paper certifying he passed the test for citizenship and, in return, he would receive a packet of materials and a flag.

185

As the official called out names, the candidates were to seat themselves in order at the front. There were about twenty-five people applying for citizenship.

I pushed the button to turn on my camera and looked around to see if others were readying to take pictures. Since we were late, I wondered if photography had been mentioned. There were only six who were not candidates for citizenship, and most of them had cameras.

* * *

As we listened to the names being called, I reflected on Dayou's phone call just after lunch. She was bubbling with excitement, saying she'd passed the test. I assumed it would be weeks before she'd be sworn in. When I asked her when the ceremony would be, she said, "At two o'clock."

"Two o'clock when?"

"Today."

After getting directions from Lady, I had changed clothes, grabbed my camera and headed for the car. In forty minutes I had driven thirty miles and found the building.

I listened to the roll call of the world: Chin, Benito, Patel, Nutriaugo, arms circling as he moved his wheelchair, Suk, Lang, Tucker. Dayou raised her hands in victory and yelled as she got up even though all the others wore silent smiles. This was an exciting event for her, one she had anticipated for months, and the inhibitions of others wouldn't keep her quiet. I walked to the front behind her to snap the first picture. When I looked at the faces of the almost-citizens, I saw their obvious pleasure in the moment.

The names went on until the last was called: Gren Costinado Johnston, Wang, Ti Buoy, Zu Ping Chang, who wore a red baseball cap and heavy coat on a day in the seventies, Chu Cheon

Chaing whose beautiful black hair spread over the collar of a red coat. Elizabeth Mary French strode forward and took the flag delicately, and, finally, Alexandria Supranchezk and Gordon Angel moved to the front.

The candidates were asked to repeat the oath. The official explained that he must see each person verbalizing it. They stood and began to speak in unison, their voices filling the room.

Did they see themselves as blessed? I was sure they did because they knew there were millions who dreamed of standing in this place and feeling the mantle of American citizenship fall over their shoulders. I hoped they were thinking about the people in history who'd risked and lost life to make this moment possible, the embattled farmers, the dough boys, the GI's, Vietnam soldiers and now our troops in Afghanistan.

I stood behind the group, so I wasn't able to see if there were any tears. But I could see the smiles when the certificates were given out.

I wanted to know their stories? I only knew one, the story of the medicine man's daughter.

Afterwards, the INS man asked them to say the Pledge of Allegiance to the flag. When they were seated, he said, "You have not given up your customs or religion. We have freedom of religion in this country. Do you know the most important right you have gained today?"

Two called out, "The right to vote."

"Yes, and if you want to know how much difference that can make, look at Florida in the last election. Register to vote and take advantage of this freedom. Your most important duty is to love this country. Don't think of yourselves as Italian-American or Chinese-American but as American because now you are, and we welcome you."

The ceremony was over, and Lady and I moved to the front of the small crowd. I hugged Dayou and congratulated her, thinking this was another milestone she and I were passing together. We waited our turn to take pictures in front of the flag. She never stopped smiling.

Dayou and Carolyn Noell at her naturalization ceremony in 2002.

* * *

The next night as President Bush began his State of the Union address, I called Dayou and asked if she was watching.

"No," she said.

I visualized the apartment. Did James have something else on or was the screen blank?

"You are a citizen now, and he is your president. You need to watch."

188

"Yeah, but you know I don't like him."

"You still need to watch."

"Maybe."

Giggling, Dayou said, "Listen to what I did to Lady. I told her she's a foreigner and that I'm a citizen now and can't be hanging out with foreigners."

"You better hush," I said, laughing. "You're terrible, Dayou. Who carried you to INS, and who gives you rides all over Charlotte?"

"I called my mother last night to tell her about the citizenship. She's still with my cousin in Monrovia. My mom asked if I passed the test and when I said, 'Yes,' she said she's so proud of me."

I heard the pleasure in Dayou's voice and realized how many times she had wanted to hear that, how many times she had cried to hear that.

"I asked my mom if she'd like to come over here," Dayou said. "She said she would, but what I think needs to happen first is that I go over there and we talk and talk and talk."

I wound the cord of the wall phone around my fingers. Often this cord has been the bond between us, and I asked myself what becoming a citizen would mean to Dayou. How would it change her life? Days ago, she said she would go home to visit even if INS had not called. Now she had an attachment that was different – a country bond.

As a child, during the war and working in Ivory Coast, Dayou was helpless. During the first years of school here, struggling to catch up and facing hepatitis, she was always at the mercy of someone else's decisions.

Now, at twenty-one, with a high school diploma, one year of community college and a job, she was looking for her first apartment. She was feeling well and has had five bonus years since surgery.

189

A caring church had modeled Christianity for her and pulled blacks and whites closer together as they met her needs. Now we were interacting and forming friendships. We often talked about the miracle of Dayou.

As an American citizen, Dayou felt for the first time that she could reach across the Atlantic to do more than visit. Maybe she could help change the quality of life for her mother and the younger children, maybe rescue her family before war broke out again.

I sensed Dayou's growing independence. Instead of asking what I thought she should do about insurance, a place to live and other matters, she took action and then told me what she'd done. My advice and help were becoming less necessary. This unexpected loss surprised me at first, and then I felt pride in her maturity.

I was touched – both by her ability to survive and her love for her family and Liberia. I saw in her the strength her mother had wanted to give her. Her father's love had gone with her from her position as the medicine man's daughter to receiving the latest in transplant technology.

As Dayou continued talking, I imagined her visit home. She and her mother would sit together for hours talking in the courtyard outside the farmhouse. When palm and rubber trees were outlined against a red sky, younger children would try to get the new sister's attention by running in and out of shadows with excited squeals.

Because of the conflicts with her mother, I wondered if Dayou had unfinished business. Maybe her longing to be with her mom was so strong because she needed to resolve the issues that had separated them. Her Aunt Meatta had raised her, yet their relationship had somehow been easier.

"Mrs. Noell," Dayou said, interrupting my thoughts. "I think I've found a place. It's near where I work."

We talked about the Williamsburg Apartments and the fact that James might move into a one-bedroom when he retired. I told her the plan sounded good.

"Call me in a few days," I said. "Now, turn on your TV, Citizen Tucker."

33

UNSETTLING NEWS

Dayou called in April, and said she needed to talk to me. I told her Tom and I would come by after church on Wednesday night. She said that would be fine. But when we got to her apartment, Dayou didn't answer the door.

When we got home, she called to apologize and said she was in the shower. I didn't buy her excuse, but didn't question her. She said she still needed to talk, and I assured her I would be available anytime she was ready.

The next day she said to me, "I have to tell you something. But you must promise not to tell Miss Debra and not to yell at me."

"Since I don't recall ever yelling at you, that part will be easy." By then, I knew what the news would be. I recalled she had been very happy for several months and had made some out of town trips with friends.

"Mrs. Noell, I'm pregnant."

We were silent for a moment. "I didn't tell you about having a boyfriend because I didn't know if it would last. He's from Liberia. His name is Richard Toe. But when I told him about the baby, he left me."

I could feel the hurt in her voice. "The other problem is that my friends told me that when you're pregnant, you shouldn't take medicines because they might harm the baby. I stopped my anti-rejection drugs."

This was scary. I didn't know if a liver transplant recipient could safely carry a child. But I knew her doctors needed to be involved immediately. Before we hung up, she promised to call the doctor's office and get in as soon as possible.

After we ended the conversation, I sat still trying to process this new information. Debra and I promised Dr. Rheindollar that she would stay on the medication regardless. I knew we were on a different and possibly dangerous path, and I couldn't guess where it would lead.

34

TRYING TO HANG ON

Wishing for Home

I'm miserable,
Mother could make medicine
from the second bark of the tree.
She could soothe my body and my soul.

May 19, 2005

As Dayou and I talked, I was thinking about her son R.J. who was now two and a half.

"Do you want your mother to raise R.J. here or take him back to Liberia?"

"I want her to stay here and let you and Miss Debra help her. But I still don't have a visa for her."

I didn't voice my question to Dayou, but wondered if Sangay would leave her children to raise a grandson in Charlotte.

Dayou's health had progressively declined during the past year. Some days were spent in the hospital; other days she had to leave work early. But through all the pain and discomfort, she was determined to care for R.J. as long as possible.

"Dayou, you know your mom doesn't have a cure."

"She has medicine for yellow jaundice that would help."

"Would you take R.J.?"

"No, Mrs.Drakeford said she'd keep him while I'm gone. You remember her."

"Yes, I know who you're talking about. Do you have any money for the air fare?"

"No, Mrs. Drakeford talked with Col. Love, my old ROTC teacher, and he wants to help, maybe with a fund raiser. She knows some other people who might help, too."

"Let me know what you need after you hear from them. But, before you go, there are some legal matters that should be taken care of. Have you talked to R.J.'s dad about relinquishing custody, so R.J. can be adopted?"

"I'm trying, but Richard hasn't returned my calls. Let me keep trying," Dayou continued. "I think maybe I can convince him. I'll tell him he won't have to pay child support if he'll sign the papers."

We were silent for a moment. "I'm so sorry about this, Dayou."

"It's okay. I can accept the fact that I can't live. But I just want a good home for my child."

I heard the intake of her breath.

We ended the conversation, and I sighed as I thought of the struggles Dayou had had and still faced. A year ago Dr. Rheindollar told us, when Debra and I went to his office with Dayou, that she was rejecting the liver, but the process was gradual and that she might have a couple of years.

He said, "She won't feel well, probably very tired, but her lab work is not too different from months back. She may need to go on disability, so I'll write a letter to that effect."

While Dr. Rheindollar was examining Dayou on the table, he said, "Dayou, have you made plans for that baby?" In a teasing way, he said, "Am I going to find him on my doorstep one morning?"

196

Dayou smiled, glanced up at him, then to the side as she said softly, "I'm making plans."

* * *

Dayou was turned down for disability. She had been able to work, and she put forth great effort to do her job because she wanted to provide what R.J. needed. Last year, she was employed in a group home for mentally handicapped adults. Now, she was a teacher in a workshop for the severely handicapped. R.J. had been in day care since he was a few weeks old.

He was a beautiful two-year-old, mentally alert, active and as strong-willed as Dayou. She'd made a choice that involved giving her life for his. While she had been pregnant, she stopped taking the anti-rejection drugs because she was afraid they would harm him. She'd had to go to the hospital, and the doctors asked her if she would allow them to abort the baby so she could take strong doses of the meds in an effort to save her liver. She refused, saying "I want to have this child, even if I die in the process. I'll take the consequences; the baby won't."

Debra and I had been with her the night she was in labor. Dayou was refusing the epidural. We had tried to persuade her to take the pain medication when we realized we didn't have to. When the pains got stronger, she would make that decision on her own. Before midnight, she was ready. The nurse suggested we go home. She said, "This is a first baby and he's not coming before sometime tomorrow."

The phone rang at six-thirty. Debra said the nurse had called saying the baby had been born about four o'clock and was doing well. I got to Dayou's room after lunch and she was holding court. Her friends from Liberia were there, and Dayou was glowing. The baby, Richard Kolo Vincent Toe, was in the nursery. There were gifts and a bouquet of balloons. I knew this was the first family member she had seen since she left Africa. But what price had she paid? Would she live long enough to know her son's personality? Would she live long enough for him to know her?

35

LAST DAYS

Death Comes on Quiet Wings

*Just let me go on,
I'm tired of being sick,
tired of the struggle.
Take care of my son.*

August 29, 2005

We had been in valleys and on hills for days before we knew on Tuesday morning that Dayou wasn't going to Chapel Hill to have a second liver transplant. On Monday she'd had a good day, and I regretted not being there because Debra said she was more like her old self. Debra said she sat on the side of the bed and asked for a hamburger and fries. Debra suggested a slushy instead, since it had been weeks since Dayou had been able to eat solid food. After lunch, Dayou became violently ill and stopped breathing. The team in ICU revived her and the doctor ordered more tests on Tuesday morning which showed an intestinal obstruction. He said she could not survive surgery with her liver and kidneys in distress. She had just gone off dialysis a couple of days before.

When I talked with Debra on Tuesday morning before leaving for the hospital, she said she had authorized removal of all life support except oxygen. Debra said, "Carolyn, I've never said this to her before, but I leaned down and whispered in her ear, 'Dayou, I love you so much, but Jesus loves you even more, and I believe it's time for you to let go and be with him. He'll put his arms around you, and there'll be no more pain. R.J. will be taken care of by Cassandra and Kelvin Drakeford as you have wanted, and you can go, knowing your plans for him are being carried out.'"

"That's good, Debra. I think you did the right thing." We were silent for a moment before I said, "Tom and I will see you in little while."

Debra had been so faithful to Dayou during this hospital stay. I was away part of the time, and sometimes Debra went home to sleep and drove back to the hospital before dawn. Dayou was not alone.

Tom and I got off the hospital elevator and passed the door of the waiting room. We no longer had to abide by the Intensive Care visiting rules since Dayou was considered to be in her last hours. Our pastor Dennis Hall was in the room with Debra and Cassandra.

I went to the side of the bed and touched Dayou's hair as I spoke to her. Her eyes were almost closed. The railings were up on her right side. I saw her blood pressure was 50/18 and mouthed the word "low" to Debra, who nodded. Tom sat in a desk-type chair a little distance from the bed. Dayou lifted her hand in greeting and opened her eyes a little, looking in his direction. The respirator and dialysis machine were gone, and she wore a clear plastic oxygen mask. The nurse came in periodically to check on her, and I asked if Dayou was receiving any medication for pain. She said that each time she had asked, Dayou had said she was not hurting. "But, I'll ask, again," she said. Gently shaking Dayou's foot, she said, "Dayou, are you in pain?"

I was surprised when Dayou opened her eyes and slightly shook her head.

The nurse said, "Meds are ordered, and whenever she needs them, we'll begin."

Tom left shortly to go to the bank and get lunch for Debra. Gennether Banks, a lady from Liberia, who keeps R.J. in her day care, came in and started crying. I put my arms around her and Dennis came over to comfort her. Cassandra spoke quietly to her, and Gennether wiped her tears.

I knew the doctors did not expect Dayou to live long since they had discontinued the medication that had been keeping her blood pressure up to acceptable levels; however, her readings were a little higher as the day progressed.

Many from R.J.'s dad's family came during the afternoon. About three o'clock, Gennether pulled out a phone card in the waiting room and said she was going to talk to Dayou's Aunt Meatta in Totota. She said Meatta didn't have a phone in her house, but she had been waiting by the booth in the street outside. Meatta had told Sangay, Dayou's mother, that Dayou was seriously ill.

When she gave the phone to me, I said I would like to speak to Meatta. "Does she have a heavy accent? Will I be able to understand her?"

"Oh, no," Gennether said. "You'll have no problem."

I said, "Meatta, I have been a friend of Dayou's for eleven years, and I want you and her mother to know that she has the best of medical care. I am so sorry her life could not be saved." I also tried to tell Meatta that I had seen a picture of her in a canoe crossing the St. Paul River to preach, but I could not understand her replies. Her voice was strong. I knew she was a forceful woman, but her pronunciation of English was so different that it was foreign to me. I gave the phone back to Gennether..

She finished the conversation and closed her cell phone. "Dayou's aunt said she couldn't understand a word you said."

"How could anyone have trouble with my southern accent?" We laughed since I had assumed I was the only one having a problem.

Wednesday was a similar day with less and less response from Dayou and many visitors coming in. At lunchtime, when I was alone with her, I stroked her arm. I read the words "Latex-free, Small Adult" on the blood pressure cuff, noted her swollen abdomen under the blue hospital gown and the chipped polish on her fingernails. I prayed aloud asking God to take her in a gentle way. I felt I was releasing Dayou to His care as I glanced down at some glamour shots of her on the floor beside Debra's pocketbook.

Debra said she was going to spend the night at the hospital. Tom and I brought supper, and I asked her to plan to go home the next morning when I got there.

Thursday morning, the hospital – preparing to receive Katrina victims – moved Dayou to a regular room on the same floor. This was appropriate since she was only getting oxygen. Tom had to deliver lunches for the senior nutrition program in Davidson, so I drove down to Charlotte alone. Debra and I sat on either side of Dayou, and we noted a change in her breathing. Her rib cage was moving up and down, and I felt she was working harder and harder to get oxygen. I glanced up at the blank TV screen and at the gold-rimmed clock with the second hand counting off the remaining time.

About eleven, the doctor came in saying UNC Hospital at Chapel Hill had called to see if she was stable enough to travel. This didn't mean a liver was available, but that she would be put on the waiting list there. Days ago, this would have been welcome news. Now, it was too late. One week before, Tom and I had been waiting in Durham for her to come to the transplant center.

Rebecca Davies, Lady's mother, came by. She worked in housekeeping on that floor. We talked about the time we tried to find her through the Liberian embassy after she got separated from her family and they came on to the states. Lois had called the embassy in D.C. seeking information about Dayou's family and Lady's mother. The officials refused to help unless the girls came up from Charlotte.

Rebecca smiled and said, "I have to go to work. May we speak to Jesus?"

Debra and I said, "Please do."

"Father, you are the author of the impossible. When we have gone as far as we can, you take over. We give Dayou into your hands to heal, if it is your will. Amen." She closed the door softly on the way out.

I took the elevator down to the café for lunch and brought a sandwich back for Debra. After eating, she went into the bathroom to get cleaned up, and five Liberian girls came into the room. One, in blue scrubs who seemed to be the leader, asked if they could pray. She wore a silver cross around her neck and silver loops in her ears. Her hair was in small braids arranged on the top of her head. We held hands, forming a circle around the bed. This reminded me of the night almost eight years ago when we had stood in a circle praying in the hall after the transplant. The girl in blue sang a song about the power of God and then prayed, saying that regardless of what humans thought, Dayou could be healed. The girls whispered prayers and said "amens" while the one next to me dropped to her knees by the bed. Each one leaned over and said a word to Dayou before leaving.

The hospice nurse entered the room. She wore a pink suit, white hose and a stethoscope. She looked at Dayou, and after appearing to consider the situation, ordered morphine. The nurse from Nigeria said she saw no indication Dayou was in pain. The hospice nurse said, "We don't know that since she's not speaking."

At 2:25 p.m., the Nigerian nurse brought in three syringes. I felt this might be the plan to help Dayou go in an easy way.

At almost 3:20, Tom called to get a report, and as he asked what time I was coming home, I saw Dayou catch a big breath. I said, "I'll talk to you later," and went to the side of the bed. Dayou didn't breathe for a little while and then grabbed one more big breath. I touched the side of her neck to see if I could feel a pulse.

"Debra, she's not breathing."

Debra left to get the nurse.

As the Nigerian nurse came to the foot of the bed, Dayou took one more breath, and the nurse nodded her head. "Yes," she said as she placed her stethoscope on Dayou's chest. Debra and I were silent.

There was a knock at the door, and Arinza, Dayou's roommate for the last two months, came in. Debra went over to hug her. Arinza sobbed as the nurse closed Dayou's eyes and pulled her chin up a little leaving her mouth slightly open.

The chaplains Jane and Michael, wearing dark suits, came in, and since Debra was black and I was not they assumed Dayou was Debra's daughter. They hugged her and Arinza and read the twenty-third psalm. I held on to the words, "Thy rod and thy staff, they comfort me."

Debra asked me to call Tom so that he could let others know, while she called Cassandra. In a few minutes our former pastor Dale Harlan was on the phone. He said, "Carolyn, you and Debra gave Dayou unconditional love. I commend you for this and for sticking by her all the way." Debra had already asked him to help with the service which would be on Sunday, so he said, "Is it okay for Carol and me to come by your house sometime Saturday?"

"Sure," I said. "We'll look forward to seeing you." Since Dale had been away from our church for four years, I knew he wanted to get current information about Dayou for the eulogy.

Arinza called to tell Tenneh, R.J.'s grandmother, who was also her grandmother, the news. She said, "Tell Old Ma, Dayou has passed and that both of her mothers are here." After closing her phone, she said, "My grandmother is upset. She didn't want to talk right now."

Paula Emrich from our church came in and gave Debra a hug. She said Pastor Dennis had been contacted.

I went back to my chair beside the bed and touched Dayou's arm. It was still warm.

"I'm going to miss you, girl. I'm going to miss you so much," I whispered as I rested my head on the side railing.

The time had a surreal quality. We had known she was dying but it didn't feel real. I moved to a chair in the corner since many Liberians were coming into the room. I remembered she had said when she was sixteen, "I want to die in my country because my family will stand around my bed." These people from Africa were her friends and her son's family, and I wondered if she would consider them an acceptable substitute?

Amregae stood next to me with her fiancée. Amergae was from Nigeria and had been at our house for Dayou's graduation party. Mario, who knew Dayou from Piedmont and West Charlotte, came in with his mother and fiancée. A young woman from Liberia with a beautiful African dress stood near the window. She wore a matching purple head wrap.

Our pastor Dennis came in, hugged Debra and me and greeted several from the Liberian community. For four hours, we stayed in the room, each person dealing with their memories, their grief. Mario told some stories about high school with Dayou, Amergae spoke quietly about memories. Some friends wiped tears silently; once or twice there was soft laughter.

I knew that for days I'd expect Dayou to call, and always there would be an empty place in my heart. I thought about R.J. He was playing this afternoon with no way to know that he would always grieve because of this moment. I thought about Sangay and Meatta in Totota and how Dayou had dreamed of visiting them, how they had molded her life.

Debra, Dennis and I walked to the parking lot together at seven-thirty, talking about what had happened during the last few days and making plans for a memorial service on Sunday.

Everything had changed, as if a curtain had fallen. I struggled to accept the fact that she was gone. I drove towards Huntersville to meet Tom for supper, feeling God's presence, but also feeling shaky.

* * *

On Sunday, September 5, 2005, people walked through early fall sun into Briar Creek Road Baptist Church to celebrate the life of Dayou. As the crowd gathered, Adelle Epps played familiar hymns on the piano. Earlier, I had placed flowers on the table at the front of the church with a butterfly perched on one leaf. The florist had added that extra touch.

Debra and I stayed in the vestibule greeting people and meeting those we did not know. There were high school friends, many from the Liberian community, Briar Creek members who had stood with Dayou through everything and James Tucker. As the pews were filled, I spotted Cassandra, Kelvin, their college-age daughter LaTavia, their high school-age son Kelvin and R.J. entering the front doors. R.J. was very shy. All of us wanted to greet him, but as a toddler, he was overwhelmed with the attention and turned to Cassandra to be held.

Debra had tee-shirts made with Dayou's picture on the front. She and several others were wearing them.

Debra, Lois, Bill, Tom and I sat near the front as Dennis Hall and Dale Harlan took places on the platform. Dennis welcomed the congregation and announced the hymn, "Great Is Thy Faithfulness." Glancing over at R.J. on Cassandra's lap, I sang the words with understanding. R.J.'s care, a great source of concern for Dayou, Debra and me, appeared to be working out in a beautiful way.

Mario Black, a friend of Dayou's from West Charlotte High, read a poem he had written, and Sharon Hall followed this with a solo of "Just a Closer Walk with Thee."

In the eulogy, Dale Harlan talked about Dayou's struggle to catch up in school, her determination to be successful. He recalled the tense days of waiting for the transplant, the night we stood together as she came out of surgery and how we prayed together.

As he talked, a slideshow of images flowed through my mind. I saw the smiling cheerleader at Piedmont Middle, the proud look when she was honored by the Charlotte City Council, her mother planting rice and lifting the water jug to her lips, bullets cutting power lines in Monrovia, a miraculous escape from a death squad at Bomi Mines, her dad's hug when they saw each other near Totota, the singing of "Mary Had a Little Lamb" in kindergarten in Ivory Coast, screams on the roller coaster at Carowinds, the love of good teachers, the struggle to stay alive when hepatitis raged, the transplant with caregivers around her, news that her family survived the war, the photograph of her Aunt Meatta crossing the St. Paul River to preach.

I could see Dayou wearing the long blue dress for the ROTC dance, friends around her at the table at her graduation party, the joy on her face when she received her mother's picture, the dark room when she learned her father was dead, elation over being in love, fear for the baby when she got pregnant, pure happiness the day R.J. was born, courage in the face of death, the request to Cassandra that she and Kelvin raise her son.

With each image, I felt grief and also thankfulness that God had let me be a part of her life. I no longer had students and our own children were out of the house, so Dayou had given a special meaning to my life. Some days, I had felt I was doing nothing significant, but in that memorial service, I realized that what I did with and for her was a valuable use of time, maybe the best use of time. I was glad I had listened to her stories about Liberia and glad I had lived a part of her life with her.

After the benediction, people greeted each other and talked quietly. I spoke to several from Liberia as I moved to the back of the auditorium. I looked back to see many stopping to speak to Cassandra and Kelvin and R.J. as others moved to the parking lot to head home.

* * *

A few days later, Octavia Baker, an associate pastor at the church, told me a butterfly came to her office window at Gordon Conwell Theological Seminary the afternoon Dayou died.

"It fluttered at the window," she said, "as if trying to get in. I was surprised since there were no flowers nearby. I noticed the butterfly because it was so persistent. It moved to the glass again and again."

"When you walked into the church with the floral arrangement," she said, "I made a connection when I saw the butterfly and remembered Thursday afternoon. I don't know that it's more than a coincidence, but it does raise a question."

After Octavia and I talked, I took the butterfly off the funeral flowers, brought it home and placed it on a table near the kitchen window. Shadows played across its wings as each day moved from morning into late afternoon. It was a constant reminder of Dayou and of the old Christian tradition that the butterfly symbolized freedom and the flight of the soul.

POSTSCRIPT

September 2013

Eight years have gone by. R.J. is being raised by Cassandra and Kelvin Drakeford. They are great parents to this bright, energetic, ten-year-old. His older brother Kelvin has finished college and his sister LaTavia married, after she graduated from college, and is now the mother of a toddler.

R.J. is a good reader. Recently, he enjoyed *To Kill a Mocking-Bird, The Help* and the movie *The Butler.* He attends Irwin Avenue Elementary School in Charlotte. Drama is a strong interest for R.J. He is enrolled in acting classes at ImaginOn.

I still recall the day Cassandra took R.J. to see Obama in 2008, the night before the election. They stood for two hours at UNCC when rain began to fall. Cassandra thought he would want to leave, but he insisted on staying. When Obama stepped on stage, Cassandra lifted R.J. to her shoulders.

He said, "I can see him, Cassie! I can see him! But I can't see his eyes. I want to see his eyes."

I love this R.J. story because it shows his intensity.

Today Cassandra says, "I know Dayou would be so proud of R.J. I just have to believe that she sees him and smiles over the young man he is becoming."

R.J.'s school photo, age 7

R.J. (left) with his cousin at his sister's wedding.

ACKNOWLEDGMENTS

I would like to thank my husband Tom Noell, who has been more than supportive and who lived this adventure beside me.

Ann Campanella edited this book and helped me prepare it for publication with the loving spirit, which is the core of her personality. I deeply appreciate Ann's attention to detail and generous gift of time in spite of her busy schedule.

Besides Ann, other members of my writers' group have listened and critiqued each chapter week after week. I give great thanks to Jean Beatty, Allison Elrod, Lisa Kline, Nancy Lammers and Judy Stacy.

My friend Jane Peck has read the manuscript several times and made many excellent suggestions.

Debra Hayes brought Dayou into my life and took care of her every time she was sick.

Special thanks to my pastor, Lib McGregor Simmons, to Jan Blodgett, archivist at the Davidson College Library and to Dale Harlan, Executive Director of Love in the Name of Christ of Mecklenburg County, who were all willing to read the book and write blurbs. Thank you. Thank you.

THE BRIDGE

A medium that transports
story from inspiration to creation.
Our desire is that authors and readers
will be affirmed through
creativity and the written word.

31335412R00133

Made in the USA
Charleston, SC
14 July 2014